THE
PLANT KINGDOM

AUTHORS

Mary Atwater
The University of Georgia

Prentice Baptiste
University of Houston

Lucy Daniel
Rutherford County Schools

Jay Hackett
University of Northern Colorado

Richard Moyer
University of Michigan, Dearborn

Carol Takemoto
Los Angeles Unified School District

Nancy Wilson
Sacramento Unified School District

Macmillan/McGraw-Hill School Publishing Company
New York   Chicago   Columbus

The mighty redwoods – tall trees, green leaves

Environmental Education:
Cheryl Charles, Ph.D.
Executive Director
Project Wild
Boulder, CO

Gifted:
Dr. James A. Curry
Associate Professor, Graduate Faculty
College of Education, University of Southern Maine
Gorham, ME

Global Education:
M. Eugene Gilliom
Professor of Social Studies and Global Education
The Ohio State University
Columbus, OH

Life Science:
Wyatt W. Anderson
Professor of Genetics
University of Georgia
Athens, GA

Orin G. Gelderloos
Professor of Biology and Professor of Environmental Studies
University of Michigan—Dearborn
Dearborn, MI

Donald C. Lisowy
Education Specialist
New York, NY

Dr. E.K. Merrill
Assistant Professor
University of Wisconsin Center—Rock County
Madison, WI

Literature:
Dr. Donna E. Norton
Texas A&M University
College Station, TX

Derrick R. Lavoie
Assistant Professor of Science Education
Montana State University
Bozeman, MT

CONSULTANTS

Assessment:
Mary Hamm
Associate Professor
Department of Elementary Education
San Francisco State University
San Francisco, CA

Cognitive Development:
Pat Guild, Ed.D.
Director, Graduate Programs in Education and
Learning Styles Consultant
Antioch University
Seattle, WA

Kathi Hand, M.A.Ed.
Middle School Teacher and Learning Styles Consultant
Assumption School
Seattle, WA

Earth Science:
David G. Futch
Associate Professor of Biology
San Diego State University
San Diego, CA

Dr. Shadia Rifai Habbal
Harvard-Smithsonian Center for Astrophysics
Cambridge, MA

Tom Murphree, Ph.D.
Global Systems Studies
Monterey, CA

Suzanne O'Connell
Assistant Professor
Wesleyan University
Middletown, CT

Sidney E. White
Professor of Geology
The Ohio State University
Columbus, OH

Macmillan/McGraw-Hill School Division
10 Union Square East
New York, New York 10003
Printed in the United States of America

ISBN 0-02-274280-8 / 6

3 4 5 6 7 8 9 RRW 99 98 97 96 95 94 93

Mathematics:
Dr. Richard Lodholz
Parkway School District
St. Louis, MO

Middle School Specialist:
Daniel Rodriguez
Principal
Pomona, CA

Misconceptions:
Dr. Charles W. Anderson
Michigan State University
East Lansing, MI

Dr. Edward L. Smith
Michigan State University
East Lansing, MI

Multicultural:
Bernard L. Charles
Senior Vice President
Quality Education for Minorities Network
Washington, DC

Paul B. Janeczko
Poet
Hebron, MA

James R. Murphy
Math Teacher
La Guardia High School
New York, NY

Clifford E. Trafzer
Professor and Chair, Ethnic Studies
University of California, Riverside
Riverside, CA

Physical Science:
Gretchen M. Gillis
Geologist
Maxus Exploration Company
Dallas, TX

Henry C. McBay
Professor of Chemistry
Morehouse College and Clark Atlanta University
Atlanta, GA

Wendell H. Potter
Associate Professor of Physics
Department of Physics
University of California, Davis
Davis, CA

Claudia K. Viehland
Educational Consultant, Chemist
Sigma Chemical Company
St. Louis, MO

Reading:
Charles Temple, Ph.D.
Associate Professor of Education
Hobart and William Smith Colleges
Geneva, NY

Safety:
Janice Sutkus
Program Manager: Education
National Safety Council
Chicago, IL

Science Technology and Society (STS):
William C. Kyle, Jr.
Director, School Mathematics and Science Center
Purdue University
West Lafayette, IN

Social Studies:
Jean Craven
District Coordinator of Curriculum Development
Albuquerque Public Schools
Albuquerque, NM

Students Acquiring English:
Mario Ruiz
Pomona, CA

STUDENT ACTIVITY TESTERS

Alveria Henderson	Andrew Duffy
Kate McGlumphy	Chris Higgins
Katherine Petzinger	Sean Pruitt
John Wirtz	Joanna Huber
Sarah Wittenbrink	John Petzinger

Red maple leaves

FIELD TEST TEACHERS

Kathy Bowles
Landmark Middle School
Jacksonville, FL

Myra Dietz
#46 School
Rochester, NY

John Gridley
H.L. Harshman Junior High School #101
Indianapolis, IN

Annette Porter
Schenk Middle School
Madison, WI

Connie Boone
Fletcher Middle School
Jacksonville, FL

Theresa Smith
Bates Middle School
Annapolis, MD

Debbie Stamler
Sennett Middle School
Madison, WI

Margaret Tierney
Sennett Middle School
Madison, WI

Mel Pfeiffer
I.P.S. #94
Indianapolis, IN

CONTRIBUTING WRITER

Jay Gartrell

ACKNOWLEDGEMENTS

Reprinted with the permission of Macmillan Publishing Company from *THE NATURE BOOK* by Midas Dekkers, illustrated by Angela de Vrede. Copyright © 1988 Midas Dekkers, Angela de Vrede and Meulenhoff Information. Translated by Jon Michael.

Reprinted with permission of Charles Scribner's Sons, an imprint of Macmillan Publishing Company from *THE ESCAPE OF THE GIANT HOGSTALK* by Felice Holman. Copyright © 1974 Felice Holman.

The Plant Kingdom

Activities!

Features

Links

Departments

Maple leaves in autumn

The Plant Kingdom

Do you like to eat pizza? Do you like to eat yogurt? What do pizza and yogurt have to do with plants? Think about what's in a pizza. It has a crust, tomato sauce, cheese, and several kinds of toppings. The crust is made from wheat flour that comes from wheat plants. The sauce is made from tomatoes that grow on tomato plants. The cheese is a dairy product that comes from cows that eat grasses. Green peppers, onions, and olives are typical pizza toppings. All of these toppings come directly from plants. Another pizza topping is pepperoni. Pepperoni is a seasoned beef and pork sausage that comes from cows and pigs. Cows and pigs eat grasses and other plants. You can see that, directly or indirectly, every part of a pizza comes from plants.

What about yogurt? Can you trace yogurt back to plants?

The paper in this book was made from cellulose fibers, which are found in all plant cell walls.

Minds On! Make a list of some of your favorite foods, clothes, and pieces of sports equipment. Share your list with two other students. Work together to trace the ingredients of these items back to plants. Use a dictionary or encyclopedia if you need help. You may not be able to trace all of the things back to plants. Some, such as water and minerals, may come from Earth's materials. Record your list and this information in your *Activity Log* on page 1. ●

These cotton bolls form from withered cotton plant flowers. Cotton is one of the most important fibers used to make clothing.

The spinning wheel was used to draw cotton into thread.

You've seen how some of your favorite foods, clothes, and sports equipment come from plants. Did you know that life on Earth also depends on plants for the oxygen in the air we breathe? It's true. You'll learn more about how plants manufacture oxygen in Lesson 2.

Humans use plants for other purposes, too. Some medicines come from plants. Malaria is a disease transmitted to humans through a mosquito bite. To treat malaria, doctors prescribe quinine that comes from the bark of a cinchona tree. Cotton from cotton plants is used to make clothing, drapes, and carpets. Wood from trees is used to make furniture and to construct buildings. Many people enjoy the beauty of the plants themselves in their homes or yards.

But why are there so many kinds of plants on Earth? In this unit, you'll explore how the different parts and processes of plants interact to carry out life functions. You'll also learn how these parts and processes allow many different kinds of plants to adapt and survive on Earth.

The bark from these cinchona tree logs will be used to produce the medicine quinine.

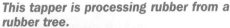

This tapper is processing rubber from a rubber tree.

This bentwood rocking chair was made from wood from a tree.

Science in Literature

In the following books, you'll see how plants and the animals that live with them can be important in people's lives. Do you know how much plants mean to the way you live? Could learning more about plants change your life for the better?

The Nature Book by Midas Dekkers. New York: Macmillan, 1988.

This lively handbook shows you how to grow the soles of your shoes to see what kinds of seeds and spores you've picked up after a day of walking around. It demonstrates the value of a fully-equipped expedition jacket you can make yourself. It tells you how to keep a friend (or an enemy!) awake with a "ticking time-bomb" of vegetable origins. You can even weave a basket out of birch twigs for yourself or a friend. Become a nature detective without a lot of expensive equipment. Become a scientist.

The Escape of the Giant Hogstalk
by Felice Holman. New York: Macmillan, 1990.

What weed can grow from seed to treetop-high overnight? It's the Giant Hogstalk! In this novel, 11-year-old Lawrence and his 20-year old cousin Anthony discover a rare plant in the Russian Caucasus Mountains and donate seeds from it to the Royal Botanic Gardens at Kew, England. Then the trouble begins. The plant grown from one of the seeds breaks the greenhouse glass one night and shoots its seeds outward. Soon all of England is covered with Giant Hogstalk plants. The weeds, whose leaves reach out to passersby and leave blisters where they grip human skin, seem almost intelligent as they resist the armies of gardeners trying to cut them down. Who will save England from this vegetable menace? Lawrence and Anthony will! But how?

Other Good Books To Read

Plants That Changed History by Joan Elma Rahn. New York: Atheneum, 1982.

Big effects may come from small causes. Would you have thought an effect as big as the Industrial Revolution could have been caused by such a seemingly small thing as people switching from firewood to coal to warm their homes? This fascinating treatment brings many different chapters of history to life.

The Marshall Cavendish Science Project Book of Plants by Steve Parker. London: Marshall Cavendish Corporation, 1986.

Splendid photographs and colorful illustrations add excitement to this handbook. With activities and little-known facts, this book provides entertainment and instruction all at once.

Greening the City Streets: The Story of Community Gardens by Barbara A. Huff. New York: Clarion Books, 1990.

In New York City on Manhattan's Lower East Side, there are 40 community gardens. This is the history of one of them, the Sixth Street and Avenue B Garden. Full-page color and black-and-white photographs light up this story of how vacant lots full of trash and weeds are turned into beautiful green spots where families can relax.

How Do

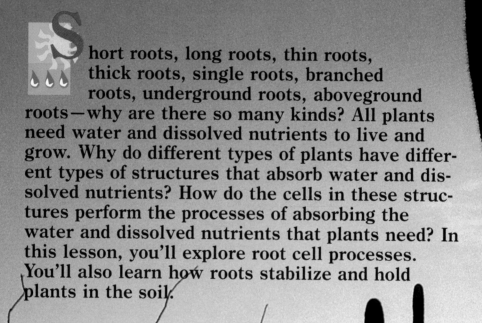

Short roots, long roots, thin roots, thick roots, single roots, branched roots, underground roots, aboveground roots—why are there so many kinds? All plants need water and dissolved nutrients to live and grow. Why do different types of plants have different types of structures that absorb water and dissolved nutrients? How do the cells in these structures perform the processes of absorbing the water and dissolved nutrients that plants need? In this lesson, you'll explore root cell processes. You'll also learn how roots stabilize and hold plants in the soil.

Plants Absorb Water and Nutrients?

Cacti can survive in desert environments because their roots spread out for large distances to absorb as much water from the infrequent rainfall as possible. Some cacti have roots that grow very deeply to absorb water that is far below the surface.

Giant redwood trees

Upturned sequoia tree showing its large root system.

Do you have any plants in your home or school? In what are these plants growing? How often do you water these plants? You know that plants need to be watered. The roots of land plants grow under the soil. Water in the soil is absorbed by plant roots. Nutrients dissolved in water in the soil are also absorbed by plant roots.

Unlike animals, plants can make their own food. They use dissolved nutrients and water from soil to help make food. Plants also need water to plump up their cells to give them support because they don't have skeletons to help support them. You'll learn more about how plants use water and dissolved nutrients to make their own food in Lesson 2.

Are there any large trees in your neighborhood, near your school, or in the park? Can you see any part of the roots of these trees? Do you have any idea how deep and wide the roots of these large trees are?

Have you ever pulled up a clump of grass or a weed? To what were the grass or weed roots attached?

Now, look at the photograph of some of the largest trees in the world—redwoods. Many of these trees grow to be 100 meters (330 feet) tall. This is almost as tall as a 30-story building! Giant sequoias, which are closely related to redwoods, can measure 30 meters (about 100 feet) around at the base. How are these trees able to grow so tall and so big around? How large do you think the root systems of redwoods need to be to hold them in the soil and absorb enough water and dissolved nutrients? Do the following Try This Activity to make a model of a tree and its roots.

Activity!

Support Structures

What You Need

large drinking straw, lump of clay, transparent tape, toothpicks, *Activity Log* page 2

Try to get your drinking straw to stand upright on your desk top. Can you do this? If you can, blow on it. Will it still stand up?

Design a way to anchor your straw so that it will stand upright even if you blow on it. Use the clay, toothpicks, and tape to help with your design. Draw this design in your *Activity Log*. Remember that roots anchor trees in the soil so that they can stand upright. If your straw represents a tree, what kind of support structures do you need to anchor it in the soil so that it won't fall over when you blow on it?

You designed a root system for a tree. Now look at some very different kinds of plants. The mosses at the bottom of this page are much smaller than a sequoia tree. Have you ever seen mosses growing on a tree trunk or on a boulder? Mosses don't have tall trunks, nor do they have roots like trees. How do mosses absorb water and dissolved nutrients? How are mosses held to the surface on which they are growing? You'll learn the answers to these questions in this lesson. You'll also discover how root cells interact to perform the processes of absorbing water and dissolved nutrients and how root systems grow to stabilize plants by anchoring them in the soil. Now, let's look at a root you are familiar with—a carrot.

How are these moss plants held to the surface of this piece of tree bark?

15

Activity!

What Are the Parts of a Root?

Did you know that a carrot is a root? The green leaves that you see on top of a carrot are the plant parts that grow above the ground. The orange carrots that you eat are the roots of carrot plants. These roots grow underground. Let's take a closer look at a carrot root.

What You Need

entire carrot plant
cross section of carrot
microscope
microscope slide
coverslip
iodine stain
dropper
laboratory apron
goggles
Activity Log pages 3–4

What To Do

1 Examine the entire carrot plant. Draw a diagram of the whole plant in your *Activity Log*. Label the part above ground and the part below ground. Do you see any small root hairs on the outside covering of the root? If so, draw and label the location of these on your diagram.

Safety!

16   See the *Safety Tip* in step 2.

will stain clothing. If it spills on your skin, flush it away with water and report it to your teacher.

3 Examine the slide under the microscope using low power. Move the slide across the field of view so that all areas of the root can be observed. Look at the outer edge of the root. Do you see small root hairs? Draw the root cross section you see under the microscope in your *Activity Log*.

4 Look for other kinds of cells. One kind should appear blue-black in color from the iodine stain. Iodine turns blue-black in the presence of starch. What do you think these cells do? Draw these cells on your root cross section diagram in your *Activity Log*.

5 Try to locate other kinds of cells in your root cross section. Draw these cells on your diagram in your *Activity Log*.

2 Place the cross section of the root on the microscope slide. Make sure to wear a laboratory apron and goggles when you work with iodine. Add 1 drop of iodine stain and a coverslip. *Safety Tip*: Iodine is poisonous and

What Happened?

1. Based on the shape of the outer cells, what do you think their function is?
2. How many cells thick are the root hairs?
3. How are the cells next to the outer cells different from the ones on the inside of the root?

What Now?

1. Predict the function of each kind of cell in your diagram and write your predictions in your *Activity Log*.
2. Design an experiment to find out where most food is stored in a carrot.

EXPLORE

Roots—Cells and Functions

You observed the cells and tissues of a carrot root in the Explore Activity. Now let's give names to the cells and tissues you identified during the activity. As you discover the names of the cells and tissues in a root and the functions of these cells and tissues, label them on your *Activity Log* diagram from the Explore Activity.

The roots of plants absorb, transport, and store water and dissolved nutrients.

Carrot plant

The root epidermis (ep´ i dur´ mis) is the outside covering of the root that comes in contact with the soil. Water and dissolved nutrients are absorbed form the soil through the root epidermis.

Cortex (kôr´ teks) cells store food. They form in the widest part of the root.

Root hairs are single, thread-like cells that are extensions of the root epidermis. Root hairs increase the surface area available for absorbing water and dissolved nutrients. Do the Try This Activity on the next page to see how many root hairs a young root has.

Xylem (zī´ ləm) and phloem (flō´ em) are tube-like tissues in some plants through which water, nutrients, and food move. Water and dissolved nutrients absorbed by the roots move through xylem up to ths stems and leaves. Food made in the leaves of plants moves through phloem to other parts of the plants that need this food.

The root cap is a dome-shaped mass of cells that protects the root as it grows and pushes its way through the soil.

The apical meristem (ā´ pi kəl mâr´ ə stem) is a dome-shaped mass of cells that divides by mitosis. These dividing cells are responsible for the growth of the root.

Cambium (kam´ bē əm) is a tissue located between xylem and phloem. Cambium tissue gives rise to new xylem and phloem tissue.

The primary root is the first part of the root to grow from a seed downward into the soil.

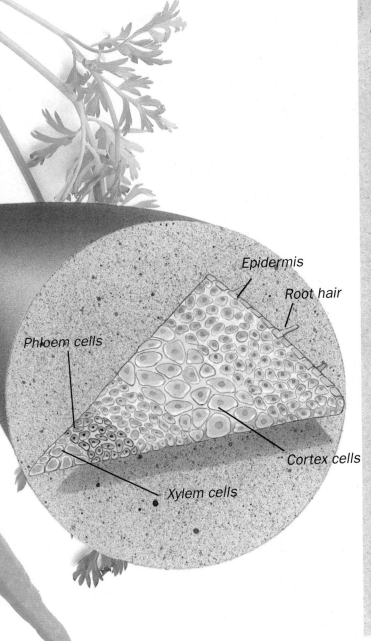

This diagram shows a wedge from a cross section of the carrot. The root cells are labeled.

Epidermis

Root hair

Phloem cells

Cortex cells

Xylem cells

Activity!

Hairy Roots

When do root hairs begin to appear on newly-growing roots? What do these root hairs look like? Do this activity to find out.

What You Need

jar, masking tape, 5 radish seeds, black construction paper, paper towel, jar lid, plastic wrap, scissors, water, hand lens, *Activity Log* page 5

Use a piece of masking tape to label the jar with your group's name. Fill the jar with water and soak 5 radish seeds in it overnight. The following day, cut a circle of black construction paper to just fit inside the bottom of the jar lid. Fold the paper towel to fit inside the jar lid and moisten it with water. Moisten the black paper with water and place it on top of the paper towel. Place your 5 radish seeds on the moist black paper. Cover the jar lid with plastic wrap and tape the wrap to the bottom of the lid securely. Label the lid with your group's name. Record the appearance of the growing roots in your *Activity Log* for each of the next 5 days. Use a hand lens to look for the root hairs. In your *Activity Log*, record an estimate of the number of root hairs on the root of each radish seed on day 5. Why do you think there are so many root hairs?

You've just seen how many root hairs are on a young radish seedling. The more root hairs a root has, the greater the surface area of the root epidermis that comes in contact with the soil. This greater surface area allows for more water and dissolved nutrients from the soil to be absorbed by the root. To see how this works, do the following Try This Activity.

Activity!

Why Are There So Many Root Hairs?

You can make a model to help you find the answer to this question.

What You Need

paper towel strips (1 10-cm x 10-cm strip, 4 1-cm x 12-cm strips), stapler, plastic cup, water, pencil, *Activity Log* page 6

Lay the 4 small paper towel strips on top of the larger strip as shown in photograph 1. Staple the 4 smaller strips to the larger strip.

Fill the plastic cup with about 3 cm of water. Lay the pencil across the rim of the cup and lay the large paper towel strip across it as shown in photograph 2. Make sure the 4 small paper towel strips hang down into the water. These paper towel strips represent a root model. Observe this root model for 20 minutes. Remove the root model from the cup. Answer the following questions in your *Activity Log*. Did the large paper towel strip absorb any water? Where did this water come from? Which parts of a root did the small paper towel strips represent? Which part of a root did the large paper towel strip represent? Why is it helpful to a plant root to have many root hairs? What do you think would happen if all of the root hairs on a plant root were damaged?

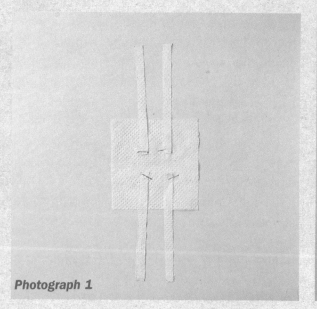

Photograph 1

Photograph 2

Minds On! Have you ever transplanted a plant from one pot to another or from a pot into the ground? Why is it important when transplanting plants to remove the plant and its roots slowly and carefully? ●

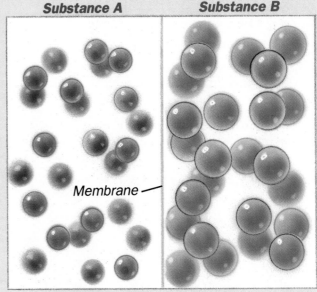

Substance A   Substance B

Membrane

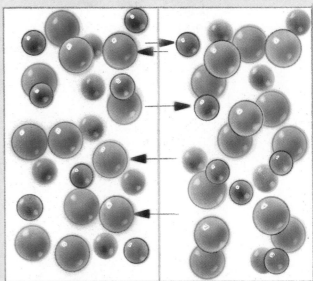

Cellular Processes in Roots

You've seen that the more root hairs a root has, the more water and dissolved nutrients it can absorb. How are water and dissolved nutrients absorbed? Root cells absorb water and nutrients by the processes of diffusion, osmosis, and active transport.

All cells are surrounded by a membrane. A cell membrane doesn't let just any and all substances pass through it. It functions something like a screen in a window, which lets air flow through but doesn't let large bugs and leaves through.

Root cells allow water, dissolved nutrients, oxygen, and carbon dioxide to pass in and out of them. You'll learn in Lesson 2 why cells need oxygen and carbon dioxide. How do these substances move through cell membranes?

Particles of matter are in constant motion. Since these particles are so small, you can't see this motion with your eyes. As a result of this motion, the particles tend to spread out evenly. This causes substances to move from regions where there are more of them to regions where there are less of them, until there are equal amounts in both regions, by a process called **diffusion**. Some dissolved nutrients diffuse through a cell membrane into a cell if there are more of these substances outside the cell than inside the cell. Likewise, some dissolved nutrients diffuse through a cell membrane out of a cell if there are more of these substances inside the cell than outside the cell.

Originally, there is more of substance A on the left side of the membrane than on the right side of the membrane. Substance A will diffuse through the membrane from the left side to the right side until there are equal amounts of substance A on both sides of the membrane. Originally, there is more of substance B on the right side of the membrane than on the left side of the membrane. Substance B will diffuse through the membrane from the right side to the left side until there are equal amounts of substance B on both sides of the membrane.

Osmosis is the process in which water diffuses through cell membranes. If there is more water outside a cell than inside a cell and there are more dissolved substances inside a cell than outside a cell, water will tend to move through the cell membrane into the cell. If there is more water inside a cell than outside a cell and there are more dissolved substances outside the cell than inside the cell, water will tend to move through the cell membrane out of the cell. Do the Try This Activity on the next page to see the general effects of osmosis.

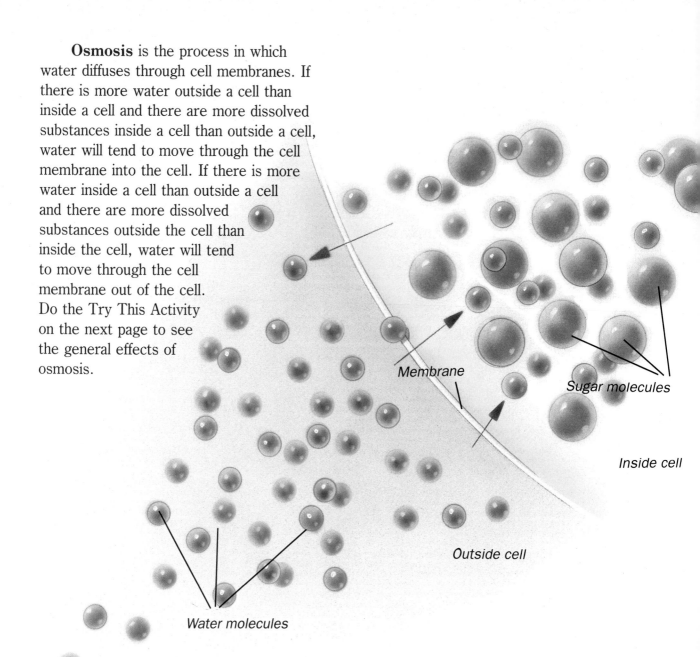

Membrane

Sugar molecules

Inside cell

Outside cell

Water molecules

There is more water outside the cell than inside the cell. There are more sugar molecules inside the cell than outside the cell. Water will diffuse into the cell by osmosis.

What if a root cell needs dissolved nutrients from the soil, even if there are more of these nutrients inside the cell than outside the cell? Diffusion would not work here. **Active transport** is the process that allows substances to move through a cell membrane into the cell even if there are more of these substances inside the cell than outside the cell. Active transport requires energy from the cell.

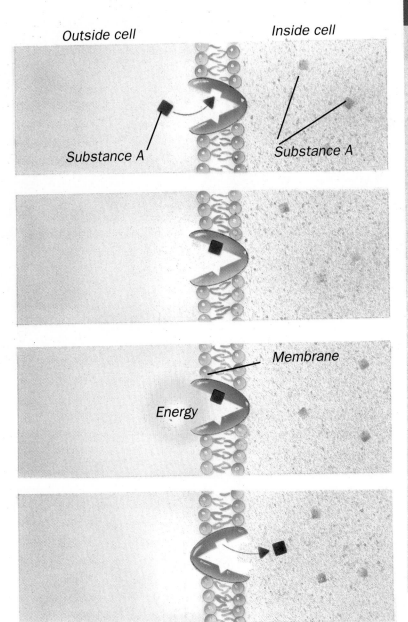

Outside cell　　　　　Inside cell

Substance A

Substance A

Membrane

Energy

Activity!

Potato Osmosis

You can see how osmosis affects a potato slice.

What You Need
2 potato slices, 2 plastic cups, masking tape, salt, plastic spoon, water, *Activity Log* page 7

Feel how firm both potato slices are. Record your observations in your **Activity Log**. Fill a plastic cup with water and label it with a piece of masking tape. Place one of the potato slices in this cup. Now, fill the other plastic cup with water and 2 large spoonfuls of salt and label it. Place the other potato slice in this cup. The next day, remove both slices and feel them. Do they feel the same? Record your observations in your **Activity Log** and explain.

There are many molecules of substance A inside the cell, but the cell still needs more of these molecules. With the addition of energy, another molecule of substance A will move into the cell by the process of active transport.

Root Systems

You've seen the cells and tissues of roots. You've learned about the processes that these cells and tissues perform. Now, let's look at the ways that roots grow and form root systems.

There are two basic types of root systems— taproots and fibrous roots. If the primary root continues to grow and becomes the plant's main root system, it's called a taproot. A **taproot** is a large single root with smaller side roots. Food is stored in the taproots of many plants. These taproots become larger as they store food. Some of this stored food is used by root cells, and some of it is later moved back up to be used by the above-ground plant parts. Some of the taproots that humans and animals eat are carrots, radishes, turnips, and beets. Pine trees also have a taproot system that can grow 6 meters (about 20 feet) or more down into the soil.

A beet is a taproot.

Fibrous roots are made up of many small branching roots that grow in clusters near the top of the soil. They spread over a large area. There is no main root. Grasses have fibrous root systems. Some maple trees and beech trees have fibrous roots. Maple and beech trees blow over easily in strong windstorms. Why do you think this can happen?

Grasses have fibrous roots.

The root systems of woody-stemmed trees often consist of a taproot with many side-branching roots. These side-branching roots help to anchor the tree in the soil so that it can stand upright and compete successfully for the sunlight it needs to make food. You'll learn more about plants' need for sunlight in Lesson 2.

The roots of most plants grow into the soil 50 centimeters to 10 meters (about 1.5–30 feet) deep. The measure of the sideways growth of root systems is often greater than the plant's height. For example, one oak tree 12 meters (about 39 feet) high had a taproot 4.7 meters (about 15 feet) deep, but its sideways roots spread out 20 meters (about 66 feet) from the base of the tree.

The root system of this tree consists of many side-branching roots to help anchor it in the soil.

Aerial roots of a tropical tree

Prop roots on a walking fig

Sometimes plants form roots on the plant parts that are aboveground. **Aerial roots** are roots that grow aboveground from the stems of plants. Many climbing vines form aerial roots that attach the climbing stems to the surface on which they are climbing. Some tropical plants form aerial roots that store dew and rainwater. **Prop roots** are aerial roots that help to support a plant.

You learned that many roots grow very deep and wide to stabilize plants and to absorb the water and dissolved nutrients that plants need to grow. How do roots grow? To answer this question, let's look at the process of mitosis.

All living organisms are made of cells. Cells are the basic units of structure and function in living organisms. A cell's hereditary information directs the growth of a cell. This hereditary information is located in the nucleus of the cell. The nucleus of a cell divides by the process of mitosis. The two nuclei that result from this division have the same hereditary information as the nucleus in the original cell. The rest of the cell also divides and is the same as the original cell. This is how roots grow—they add more cells at the apical meristem by the process of mitosis.

Roots can help prevent soil erosion.

You've seen how roots can grow very deep and wide into the soil. How can root systems affect the soil in which they are growing? Roots can help prevent soil erosion, make soil more fertile, and even help make new soil by breaking up rocks. Most grasses have fibrous root systems that are made up of a network of many small roots spreading out in all directions. Roots like this aren't strong enough to support large, tall plants, but they are good at absorbing water and dissolved nutrients in dry or sandy soils. Large nets of fibrous roots slow erosion by holding the soil in place. This prevents the soil from blowing away during high winds or washing into streams and rivers when it rains.

The fibrous roots of grass help to hold soil in place.

Have you ever seen a plant growing in a crack in a rock or pushing through a concrete sidewalk? The roots of some plants can grow into tiny cracks in rocks. The force that results from the growth of these roots widens the cracks slightly and lets water into the rocks. The force from growing roots and the action of freezing and melting water further breaks down the rocks. Dead roots decay and add decaying matter to the rock fragments. As years go by, the process of breaking solid rocks into smaller and smaller pieces and mixing the rock fragments with decayed plant matter forms new soil.

You've learned about roots of plants that have xylem and phloem tissues. Plants that contain tubelike tissues (xylem and phloem) are called **vascular** (vas′ kyə lər) **plants.** Plants that don't have tubelike tissues (xylem and phloem) are called **nonvascular plants.**

Rhizoids—Cells and Functions

Nonvascular plants don't have xylem and phloem tissues that move water, dissolved nutrients, and food through them. Do nonvascular plants have roots?

The roots of this tree have broken up this rock.

Mosses are nonvascular plants that are generally less than 20 centimeters (about 8 inches) long. Water and nutrients enter mosses directly through the stemlike and leaflike parts. Because mosses don't have tubelike tissues that transport the substances they need to live and grow, they can't grow as large or as tall as vascular plants. Mosses don't have roots. They have structures called rhizoids. **Rhizoids** (riz′ oydz) are long, single cells that attach the moss to the surface on which it is growing.

These moss plants have rhizoids to anchor them in place.

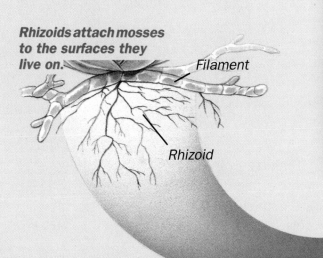

Rhizoids attach mosses to the surfaces they live on.

Filament

Rhizoid

How Do Humans Use Roots?

You've learned how roots function to keep plants living. Now let's see how roots are used by humans.

Health Link

Roots Are Good Food!

As you've learned, many plants store food in their roots. Some of the foods you eat are actually plant roots. Examples are carrots, parsnips, turnips, sugar beets, and sweet potatoes.

It's important to have a well-balanced diet that includes vitamins and minerals. Let's look at the vitamins and minerals in some roots. Pick at least one vitamin and one mineral listed below and research its benefits.

The numbers listed are IUs. IUs stands for International Units, which are agreed-upon units that produce a particular biological effect.

Vitamins	Whole Raw Carrot	Boiled Parsnip	Boiled Turnip
Vitamin A	20250.000	0.000	0.000
Vitamin B6	0.106	0.073	0.053
Vitamin B12	0.000	0.000	0.000
Vitamin C	6.700	10.100	9.050
Vitamin D	—	—	—
Vitamin E	0.472	1.155	0.36
Minerals			
Calcium	19.000	29.000	17.150
Magnesium	11.000	23.000	6.250
Potassium	233.000	287.000	105.500
Sodium	25.000	8.000	39.000

For the next five days, keep a list in your *Activity Log* on page 8 of all the roots you eat. Explain the benefits of the vitamin and mineral you researched, and tell how you are getting the benefits of this vitamin and mineral by eating roots.

Roots are also used as spices and in herbal remedies. Herbal root remedies are preparations of roots that are thought to help people who are suffering from some kind of discomfort or disease. Not everyone agrees that herbal root remedies are helpful. Some doctors believe they are helpful, and others don't. Most people decide whether they are helpful or not after they have tried these herbal roots themselves!

Root Spices

Do you like spicy foods? What kinds of spices do you like? Have you ever tasted horseradish? Horseradish is a very hot spice. It is made from the root of the horseradish herb. Freshly grated horseradish root is so spicy that it causes many people's noses to run!

Horseradish root is also used as an herbal medicine. It's a very good source of vitamin C and has also been used to treat asthma and coughs.

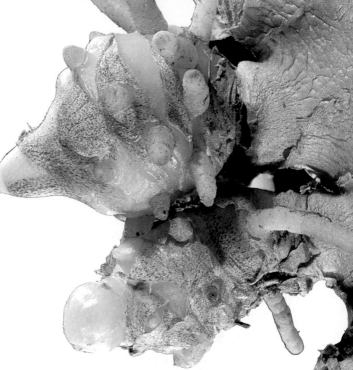
Ginger root is used as a spice and as an herbal medicine.

Horseradish root is used to make horseradish sauce.

GLOBAL PERSPECTIVE

"Root of Life"

The root of the ginseng plant is sometimes called Root of Life, Root of Immortality, and Man Root. The ginseng root is shaped somewhat like a human body. It looks like it has a head region, two arms, and two legs. This is why it's sometimes called Man Root.

The root of the ginseng plant is harvested and used as a natural herbal medicine by many people. Ginseng is native to North America and China. Several Native American tribes have used ginseng root to treat stomach disorders, headaches, fevers, and coughs. The Chinese have used ginseng root to treat diabetes, blood and blood vessel disorders, and stomach disorders.

The root of the ginseng plant isn't ready to harvest until the entire plant has been growing for six or seven years. The root is said to get better as it gets older. An excellent root is produced by a nine-year-old ginseng plant. Several 400-year-old ginseng plants have been found!

The Chinese and Koreans have designed an interesting way of preparing ginseng roots after harvest. They clean the fresh roots and then place them in a basket that is put in a closed earthenware steamer. This steamer is placed on top of an iron pot of boiling water. The roots are steamed for one to four hours and then carefully dried over a slow-burning wood fire. After seven to ten days, the dried roots are hard and brittle and are colored dark red. Roots prepared this way are called Red Ginseng.

Ginseng plant and root

Ancient Chinese Legend

An ancient Chinese legend tells of a group of ginseng root hunters. According to this legend, the ginseng root shines and moves around by itself at night. The hunters used tiny bows and arrows to hunt ginseng roots at night. Only with tiny arrows that had strings attached to them were these hunters able to catch the glowing, moving roots.

A researcher at the United States Department of Agriculture Economic Botany Laboratory decided to challenge this legend. The researcher planted 100 ginseng plants in an experimental garden. The next morning the researcher found that almost half of the ginseng roots had moved out of the holes they had been planted in, but the roots had not been eaten! The researcher replanted the ginseng and again found that about half of the plants had been disturbed during the next night. The researcher couldn't prove the legend wrong. Can you think of any other experiments this researcher could do to test whether the roots move overnight?

Sum It Up

Unlike animals, plants can make their own food. To do this, they need to take in water and dissolved nutrients from the soil through their roots. The different cells and tissues of a root interact to allow the root to carry out its functions. In the Explore Activity, you saw cells of root hairs, epidermis, xylem, phloem, cortex, cambium, apical meristem, and root caps. These cells perform the processes of osmosis, diffusion, and active transport that allow the water and nutrients to move into the root from the soil. These substances then move upward through the xylem to the leaves where they are used to make food. Plant roots function to stabilize plants by anchoring them in the soil. Humans enjoy plant roots as foods, spices, and herbal remedies.

Powdered ginseng root is often used in teas.

Critical Thinking

1. When plant nursery workers remove plants from the ground, why do they often leave a ball of soil around the roots?

2. What kind of root system do you think trees that are easily uprooted by wind have? Why?

3. What do you think would happen if you placed a slice of potato in distilled water?

4. Why do mosses grow in moist areas?

5. A plant growing in soil that has a small amount of potassium will get potassium from the soil even though there is more potassium inside the root cells than there is in the soil. Explain how this happens.

How Do Plants Make, Transport, Store, and Use Food?

Sunlight, plant leaves, food, energy— how are these related? All living organisms need food. Plants produce food. Plants and animals use the food made by plants to produce the needed energy to support life functions. In this lesson, you'll learn how plant cells work together as systems to produce and use food.

Have you ever been inside a greenhouse? If so, what did you see? How did it smell inside the greenhouse? How did it feel? Was it warm or cool? Humid or dry? Describe the greenhouse to your classmates.

Now, look at the photograph of the greenhouse on these two pages. How would you describe this greenhouse? What kind of material was used to make the walls and ceiling? Why do you think this material was used? Can you see anything sticking to the walls and ceiling? Where do you think this substance comes from? Can you recognize any of the plants in this greenhouse? Are any of them plants that you have eaten?

Greenhouses are controlled environments providing plants the best conditions in which to grow. In a greenhouse, you can often find plants with large leaves and plants with small leaves, plants with long stems and plants with short stems, plants with flowers and plants with pine cones. You can design your own greenhouse in the activity below.

Think about the things you already know about plants. You know that, unlike animals, plants can make their own food. You know that plant roots and rhizoids absorb water and dissolved nutrients from the soil. Plants also need sunlight. In this lesson, you'll discover how plants use water, dissolved nutrients, and sunlight, as well as carbon dioxide and oxygen, to make food and use it to live and grow. You'll also learn about the different leaf and stem cells and tissues that work together as systems to perform the processes of making, transporting, and using food.

Now let's explore how plants use carbon dioxide.

Activity!

Design Your Own Greenhouse

Plants have specific requirements for growth. Use what you already know about these requirements and research several types of greenhouses to help you design your own greenhouse.

What You Need
reference books, *Activity Log* page 9

Use a reference book to research greenhouses. Then, work with a partner to design and draw a greenhouse in your *Activity Log*. Draw the plants you would like to have in your greenhouse. List the specific requirements the plants in your greenhouse will need to grow. For example, your plants will need to be watered, so water is one requirement. Share your design with the class.

Activity!

Plants in the Light, Plants in the Dark

When do plants use carbon dioxide? Do this activity to find out.

What You Need

16 oz jar
3 test tubes with caps
plastic drinking straw
2 *Elodea* sprigs (kept in the dark for 2 days)
light source
scissors
aluminum foil
masking tape
bromothymol blue solution
dropper
plastic cup
goggles
laboratory apron
plastic gloves
Activity Log pages 10-11

What To Do

Work in groups of four. Share responsibility to complete each of the following steps.

1 Fill the plastic cup with bromothymol blue solution.

2 Have one person in your group use the plastic drinking straw to exhale into the solution. *Safety Tip:* Do not inhale the solution through the straw. Observe the color of the solution as the group member exhales. This group member should continue to exhale until the color of the solution stops changing. Record your observations in your *Activity Log*.

3 Use masking tape to make the following labels for the 3 test tubes.
1 bromothymol solution
2 bromothymol solution and *Elodea* sprig
3 bromothymol solution and *Elodea* sprig (test tube covered with aluminum foil)

Safety!

See the *Safety Tip* in step 2.

4 Use the scissors to cut off a few cm from the bottom of each sprig of *Elodea.* Place one sprig into test tube 2 and the other into test tube 3.

5 Use the bromothymol solution into which one of the group members exhaled in step 2 to fill each test tube. Place the caps into each tube. Record the color of each solution in your *Activity Log*.

6 Remove the label from test tube 3. Wrap test tube 3 completely with aluminum foil so that light can't enter the tube. Reapply the label over the aluminum foil.

7 Place all test tubes in the jar and put them where they will receive light from an indoor light source.

8 The next day, examine the test tubes. Record the color of the solution in each test tube in your *Activity Log*.

What Happened?

1. At the very start of the experiment, a group member exhaled into the bromothymol blue solution. What gas was this person exhaling? What color change occurred to the solution as the person exhaled? What do you think this color change indicated?

2. Did the solution in any of the test tubes change color overnight? If so, what color change occurred? What was in the test tube or tubes that changed color? What do you think this color change indicates? What conditions did these tubes experience?

3. Did the solution in any of the test tubes fail to change color overnight? If so, what was in the test tube or tubes that did not change color? What conditions did these tubes experience?

What Now?

1. What can you infer based upon the test tube or tubes that changed color overnight?

2. What conclusion can you draw based on the test tube or tubes that didn't change color overnight?

3. Design an experiment to find out if the solution in the test tube or tubes that changed color overnight can be made to change back to the original color. Explain your observations in your *Activity Log*.

EXPLORE

Photosynthesis—the Process of Making Food

In the Explore Activity, you saw that in the presence of light, plants use carbon dioxide gas. Plants use carbon dioxide gas, water, and energy from sunlight to make food in the process of **photosynthesis**.

*Just inside the upper epidermis is the layer of **palisade cells**. The palisade cells are loosely packed and contain chloroplasts.*

You saw that greenhouses are made of transparent material so that sunlight can reach the plants inside. How do plants capture the energy from sunlight? A structure called a **chloroplast**, found in plant cells, contains chlorophyll. **Chlorophyll** is a green pigment. A **pigment** is a substance that absorbs light. Plant leaves appear green because chlorophyll absorbs most of the sun's visible light wavelengths except green light wavelengths. Because most green light wavelengths aren't absorbed by chlorophyll, they are reflected by the leaves of plants and reach our eyes. This is why plants that contain chlorophyll look green. The visible light wavelengths that are absorbed by chlorophyll provide the energy needed for photosynthesis. Chloroplasts contain pigments other than chlorophyll. These pigments also absorb visible light wavelengths from sunlight that

*The upper surface of a leaf, called the upper **epidermis**, is made of a thin layer of brick-shaped cells. The cells of the epidermis don't usually have chloroplasts. A layer of a waxy substance called the **cuticle** (kū´ ti kəl) covers the epidermis of some leaves. This waxy cuticle keeps the leaf from losing too much water.*

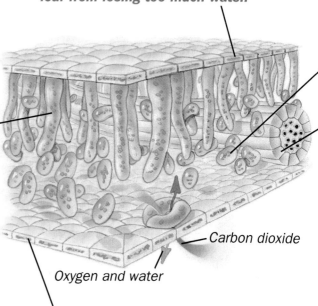

Carbon dioxide

Oxygen and water

*The lower surface of a leaf is called the lower **epidermis**. The lower epidermis usually contains guard cells which surround openings called stomata. Carbon dioxide diffuses into leaves through open stomata and oxygen and water diffuse out of leaves through open stomata.*

This leaf cross section shows that plant leaves are made up of several kinds of cells.

contribute some energy for photosynthesis. Some of these pigments absorb different wavelengths of visible light than chlorophyll does. Therefore, these pigments allow different wavelengths of light, other than green, to reach our eyes. Do the Try This Activity on the next page to see chlorophyll and other pigments that chloroplasts contain.

Just inside the lower epidermis is the layer of spongy cells. The spongy cells are more loosely packed than the palisade cells and also contain chloroplasts. There are many air spaces between the cells in the spongy layer.

The bundles of xylem and phloem form the **veins** that run through the spongy layer. Water from the stem enters a leaf through the veins. Food made in a leaf moves out of the leaf through the veins.

Activity!

What Pigments Are Found in Leaves?

Do this activity to see chlorophyll and some of the other pigments in plant leaves.

What You Need

green leaf from an outdoor plant, coin, 16 oz jar, chromotography paper, fingernail polish remover, pencil, transparent tape, *Activity Log* page 12

1. Lay the green plant leaf across one end of the chromotography paper about 15 mm from the end. Rub the edge of a coin back and forth over part of the leaf several times until a thick green line appears on the paper.
2. Pour 5 mm of the polish remover into the jar. *Safety Tip:* Do not breathe the fumes of fingernail polish remover. Keep the polish remover away from eyes. Wash hands after using the remover. Return capped polish remover bottle to your teacher when finished.
3. Tape the chromotography paper to the pencil and hang it so the end with the green leaf rubbing is just above the polish remover, but not in it. The polish remover will be absorbed by the paper and will move up the paper strip. Leave the chromotography paper in the polish remover for 10 minutes.

Answer the following questions in your *Activity Log*. What color was the line where the leaf was rubbed before the chromotography paper was placed in the polish remover? What happened to the line after the chromotography paper was placed in the polish remover? What colors were on the chromotography paper after it was left in the polish remover for 10 minutes? Where were these colors located on the chromotography paper? Could you see these colors in the leaf?

Do you live in a climate where some leaves change color in autumn? What are some colors of autumn leaves? During autumn, there are fewer hours of daylight—there is less time that the sun shines. Less available sunlight causes changes in plant hormones (chemical messengers). These changing plant hormones can cause chlorophyll to break down. When chlorophyll is broken down, the plant leaves will no longer appear green. Chlorophyll must be present in plant leaves for photosynthesis to occur. The energy from the light wavelengths absorbed by chlorophyll is necessary for carbon dioxide and water to combine to form food. However, the other pigments that you saw in the Try This Activity remain in the plant leaves. These pigments, along with other pigments that form in leaves in autumn, are responsible for the colors of autumn leaves.

When carbon dioxide and water combine by using the light energy absorbed by chlorophyll, sugar and oxygen form.

What causes the different colors of these leaves?

$$\text{carbon dioxide + water} \xrightarrow{\text{light energy}} \text{sugar + oxygen}$$

Sugar is the basic unit of food produced by plants. Food not immediately used by plants can be stored in roots, stems, leaves, fruits, and seeds. The oxygen becomes part of the air we breathe. Animals and plants use the food and oxygen formed by the process of photosynthesis.

Leaves are a plant's main "solar energy collectors." The leaves of many kinds of plants have a large surface area available to absorb the sun's energy. In addition to the sun's energy, carbon dioxide and water must also be available in the leaf for photosynthesis to occur. How do these substances get into a leaf?

The leaves of land plants obtain carbon dioxide from the surrounding air by diffusion. The surrounding air has more carbon dioxide than the leaf, so carbon dioxide gas diffuses into the leaf through openings called **stomata** (singular—stoma) in the epidermis of the leaf. Leaves usually have more stomata on the lower epidermis than on the upper epidermis. The word *stoma* comes from the Greek word meaning "mouth." Do stomata look like mouths? Green stems can also have stomata. Stomata open into the air spaces inside the leaf. Each stoma is surrounded by two cells called **guard cells**. Do the following Try This Activity to find out how guard cells function to allow substances into and out of a leaf.

Activity!

How Do Stomata Open and Close?

Guard cells can swell and shrink. You can see this happen and see how it affects the stomata.

What You Need

hand lens, lettuce leaf, distilled water, dropper, forceps, microscope slide, coverslip, microscope, salt water, paper towel, watch, *Activity Log* page 13

1. Observe the upper and lower surfaces of the lettuce leaf with the hand lens.
2. Tear a 5-cm square from the lettuce leaf. Bend this square in half, then use the forceps to remove the thin layer of epidermis from the leaf.
3. Use the dropper to place a drop of distilled water onto the microscope slide. Make sure the slide and coverslip are clean. Place the thin layer of epidermis you removed from the lettuce leaf on the drop of water and place a coverslip over it. Observe the epidermis layer using the microscope at low power.
4. Observe the epidermis and locate a pair of kidney-bean-shaped guard cells and a stoma. Draw the epidermis, guard cells, and stoma in your *Activity Log*.
5. Now, use the dropper to place a drop of salt water by the edge of the coverslip. Use the paper towel to draw the salt water under the coverslip by touching the paper towel to the side of the coverslip opposite the drop of salt water. Wait about 5–10 minutes, then observe the epidermis using the microscope at low power. In your *Activity Log*, draw the epidermis, guard cells, and stoma as they appear after coming in contact with salt water.

In your *Activity Log*, describe how guard cells are different from the other cells of the epidermis. How do the changes in guard cells that come in contact with the salt water affect the stomata? Do you recall the "Potato Osmosis" Try This Activity from page 23 of Lesson 1? Relate osmosis to the changes in the guard cells.

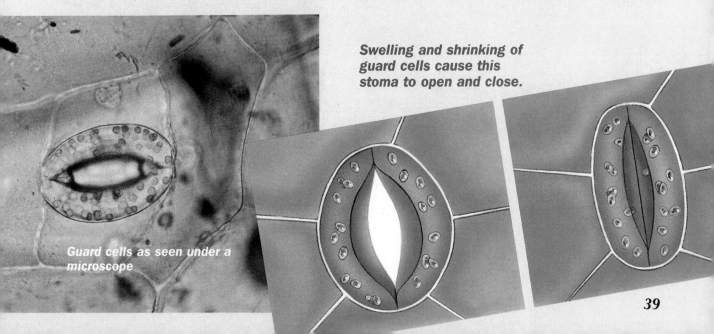

Swelling and shrinking of guard cells cause this stoma to open and close.

Guard cells as seen under a microscope

39

When guard cells absorb water by osmosis, they swell. In the Try This Activity, you saw how this swelling caused the stomata to open. When stomata are open, carbon dioxide gas can diffuse into leaves. The oxygen gas that's produced by photosynthesis can also move out of leaves through open stomata. When guard cells lose water by osmosis, they shrink. In the Try This Activity, you also saw how this shrinking of guard cells caused stomata to close. When stomata are closed, carbon dioxide gas and oxygen gas can't move into and out of leaves.

You learned in Lesson 1 that water moves into root hairs by the process of osmosis. In vascular plants, water in the root hairs moves into the xylem of the root that is connected to the xylem of the stem. Water then moves upward through the xylem in the root and stem into the xylem of the leaves. The leaves of many plants are connected to stems by structures called **petioles**. The leaves of some plants such as grass don't have petioles. Petioles contain xylem and phloem that are continuous with xylem and phloem in stems and connect to the xylem and phloem bundles in leaves that make up veins. Water moves from the xylem in leaves to the other cells in the leaves. Once water is in cells that contain chlorophyll, it can be used in the process of photosynthesis.

The vascular bundles (xylem and phloem) are continuous through the stem, petiole, and leaf.

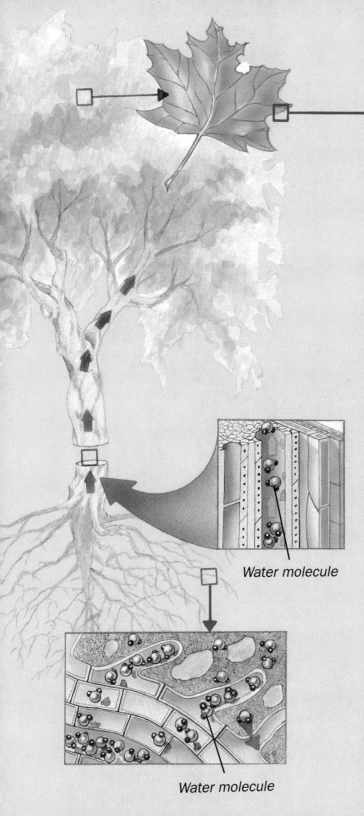

Water molecule

Water molecule

Water molecule

Water enters the roots of a tree, moves upward through the xylem, and can diffuse out through open stomata.

So you see that three things are needed for photosynthesis to take place. When light is absorbed by chlorophyll in a leaf, when the stomata are open allowing carbon dioxide gas into the leaf, and when water is available in the cells of the leaf, photosynthesis can occur. Can photosynthesis occur at night? Why or why not?

There is another activity that occurs when leaf stomata are open. When the stomata on a leaf are open, allowing carbon dioxide gas to diffuse into the leaf, water can diffuse out of the leaf through open stomata by the process of **transpiration**. As the water diffuses out of the leaf, it evaporates. Evaporation is the change of water from liquid to water vapor. Do you remember the picture of the greenhouse on the second page of this lesson? You saw moisture on the walls and ceiling of the greenhouse. Where do you think this moisture came from? Transpiration decreases the amount of water in the leaf. The plant will need to absorb more water from the soil through its roots to make up for the water lost by transpiration. The process of transpiration is responsible for the absorption of water from the soil by roots and the upward movement of water in the xylem of roots, to the xylem in stems, and to the xylem in leaves.

Stem Support

You've seen why leaves are important for plants—they provide a place for photosynthesis to take place. Why are stems important for plants?

Stems provide support for leaves. Stems also provide pathways for the movement of water from the roots up to the leaves and for the movement of food from the leaves to other parts of the plant.

Stems have the same kinds of tissues as roots. Xylem is continuous from the root, through the stem, through the petiole, and through the leaf. Phloem is also continuous through all of these plant parts. Food made in the leaves of plants moves to the other parts of plants through the phloem. Xylem and phloem are separate conducting tubes.

Xylem

Phloem

The xylem and phloem in herbaceous plant stems are arranged in bundles.

The xylem and phloem in woody-stemmed plants are arranged in two separate rings—the xylem ring is inside the phloem ring.

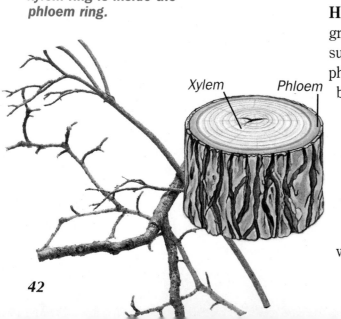

Xylem   *Phloem*

There are two kinds of stems. **Herbaceous** (hûr bā´ shəs) **stems** are green and soft. They are found in plants such as tulips and tomatoes. Xylem and phloem in herbaceous stems are arranged in bundles. **Woody stems** are rigid and hard. Woody stems are found in trees and shrubs. They have a lot of xylem tissue. The xylem tissue becomes the wood of the tree. Xylem and phloem in woody stems are arranged in two separate rings with the xylem ring inside the phloem ring. The tissue outside of the wood is called the bark.

Minds On! In your *Activity Log* page 14, make a list of the plants in your yard or by your school that have herbaceous and woody stems. Note which of the plants on your list are the tallest, then answer the following question. Do herbaceous plants or woody-stemmed plants grow taller? ●

Many land plants can grow tall because water, dissolved nutrients, and food can move great distances through the large network of xylem and phloem. Do the Math Link to get an idea of how tall some trees can grow.

Which of these plants have herbaceous stems and which have woody stems?

Math Link

Tall Trees

How tall can trees grow? Here are amazing heights that some trees have reached!

Do you know the average height of humans? Research this fact, then figure out how many average-humans tall each of the trees listed below is. In your *Activity Log* page 15, make scale drawings showing the number of humans, stacked foot to head, needed to reach the same height as each of these trees.

California redwood	110 m	(about 365 ft)
cedar tree	66 m	(about 220 ft)
beech tree	48 m	(about 160 ft)
cottonwood tree	44 m	(about 145 ft)

Respiration—the Process of Getting Energy From Food

Xylem and phloem cells, as well as the other cells in leaves and stems, grow by the process of mitosis. The energy from food must be available to all living and growing cells.

How do plants use the food that is made in their leaves? Plants get energy from food through the process of respiration. **Respiration** is the process of obtaining energy by using sugar and oxygen, which go through a series of chemical reactions to produce carbon dioxide, water, and energy.

sugar + oxygen $\longrightarrow$
carbon dioxide + water + energy

Sugar and oxygen are the end products of photosynthesis. Plants and animals use the end products of photosynthesis to produce energy through respiration. Photosynthesis occurs only in cells that contain chlorophyll. Respiration occurs in all living cells of all living organisms.

You remember that dissolved nutrients from the soil are absorbed by roots and move up to the leaves of plants. These nutrients aren't used as food by plants. They are chemicals—other than carbon dioxide, oxygen, and water—that are required by a plant. Some of these chemicals are nitrogen, potassium, calcium, phosphorous, and sulfur. These chemicals combine with sugar from photosynthesis to form cell-building materials, as well as several other substances needed by plants.

Minds On! Have you ever used "plant food" on your houseplants or in your garden? Get a bottle or box of "plant food" from your teacher or from your home and find out what the ingredients are. List these ingredients in your *Activity Log* page 16. How are these ingredients used by plants? Is the label "plant food" really correct? ●

Have you ever heard of a Giant Hogstalk plant? This fictional plant will never need a drop of "plant food"! To find out why, read the Literature Link below.

Literature Link

The Escape of the Giant Hogstalk

"All he was doing was ambling—just ambling, nothing more—when quite suddenly an absolutely enormous thing seemed to leap out at him from the bushes. His first thought was that it was an animal and that he was unarmed and without so much as a cookie to charm it. But when he had cowered back from it and could view it more calmly at a slight distance, he saw that it was a plant—but such a plant! Fifteen feet or so in height! Six inches, anyway, across the stalk, upon which grew great finger-like leaves which *clutched*. And topping all this were the most enormous flower heads he had ever seen."

In Felice Holman's novel *The Escape of the Giant Hogstalk,* a species of giant weeds nearly takes over England. Sketch your idea of what a Giant Hogstalk looks like, and write a story or a skit about the weed. Is it intelligent? Does it take over the world? If not, how does your main character control its fantastic growth? Use what you know about plant growth to make your writing as realistic as possible.

Each bunch of moss growing on this tree consists of many tiny individual moss plants.

The transport of water, dissolved nutrients, and food through xylem and phloem makes it possible for these trees to grow so tall.

Nonvascular plants make and use food by the same processes, photosynthesis and respiration, that vascular plants use to make and use food. However, nonvascular plants do not have xylem and phloem tissues to transport water, dissolved nutrients, and food throughout the plants.

Mosses are nonvascular plants. Some mosses have food-conducting cells through which food can move. However, these food-conducting cells don't form large conducting tubes. They don't make up true vascular tissue. They can't move food long distances, which is why mosses don't grow

very large. You may remember that an individual moss plant is usually less than 20 centimeters (about 8 inches) tall. Compare this to giant sequoia trees that grow to be 100 meters (about 330 feet) tall! How much taller is a sequoia tree than a moss?

45

Falling Leaves

You've learned that leaves are important plant structures. Photosynthesis occurs in leaves. Do the same leaves stay on a tree for the entire life of the tree? You've probably seen leaves fall from trees or seen pictures of bare trees. The yearly life cycle of many plants in cool and cold regions of Earth involves a shutdown of growth, or a period of **dormancy.** The shorter and cooler days of autumn affect plant hormones. The changing plant hormones cause the materials in the cells of the petiole and leaf to break down. When an area of cells at the base of the petiole breaks down, the leaf will fall from the stem of the tree. In the spring, when warmer temperatures and longer days return, new leaves develop and the growth cycle begins again.

Budding leaves on a red maple tree

Healthy, growing leaves on a red maple tree

Dying leaves on a red maple tree

Do you know what an evergreen tree is? The pine tree shown in the photograph on this page is an evergreen tree. Does an evergreen tree lose its leaves or does it stay ever green? **Evergreen trees** such as pine trees and fir trees lose their needle-shaped leaves gradually. Therefore, evergreen trees are never completely without leaves and appear to be ever green. If you've walked through woods filled with pine trees, you've seen the floor of the woods covered with brown needles. These brown needles fell from pine trees and were replaced by new green needles.

But what about trees that lose all their leaves in a short period of time? These trees are called deciduous trees. **Deciduous** (di sij´ ü əs) **trees** such as oak trees and maple trees lose all their leaves at the end of each growing season.

If you were planning to decorate the grounds around your home or school with trees, would you want to plant evergreen trees or deciduous trees? Landscape architects need to make these kinds of choices all the time. You can read about a landscape architect's career on this page.

These brown needles gradually fall from an evergreen tree.

Landscape Architect

A landscape architect designs and develops land for people's use and enjoyment. A landscape architect may design a small garden, a city plaza, a playground, a shopping mall, or part of a national park.

A landscape architect designing a city plaza may include a fountain, seating areas, and various kinds of ornamental plants. The landscape architect would need to know the kinds of plants that grow best in different climates and the kinds of plants that look best in different environments. He or she also needs to study the environment the plants will be inhabiting—is it windy? Sunny? Shaded? Damp?

A landscape architect needs to know much about plants, as well as about water supply, climate, soil, and landforms. Most jobs as a landscape architect require a college degree. Classes in botany (the study of plants), geology, and landscape art and design are required for a college degree in landscape architecture.

A landscape architect designs gardens and yards such as this.

The common mullein is a biennial plant.

Sunflowers are annual plants.

Do some plants live longer than others? A landscape architect would need to know the life span of many kinds of plants. **Annual plants** grow, reproduce, and die within one growing season. Can you name any annual plants that you may have planted in a garden? **Biennial plants** produce leaves and food in one year and reproduce and die in the second year. Cabbage and carrot plants are biennial plants you may have seen. **Perennial plants** live from one growing season to another. Are woody-stemmed plants annual, biennial, or perennial? Do the following Try This Activity to find out.

Blue violets are perennial plants.

TRY THIS # Activity!

Rings Around Plants

Can you tell how many growing seasons a tree has had?

What You Need
cross section of a tree branch, hand lens, *Activity Log* page 17

Count the number of rings on your tree branch. Record this number and sketch the tree cross section in your *Activity Log*. Form a hypothesis about what the rings in your tree cross section are. Are all the rings the same width? Measure the widest and narrowest rings and note these in your *Activity Log*. Why might a tree grow a thick ring one year and a thinner ring the next year?

Annual growth rings form in woody-stemmed plants. Each year as the thickness of the stem increases, a circle of wood (xylem tissue) called a growth ring is added. In wet years, growth rings are wide. In dry years, growth rings are narrow. The age of some woody-stemmed plants can be found by counting the annual growth rings.

Growth rings on tree stumps

Sum It Up

The systems and interactions of plant cells, along with carbon dioxide and water, provide the food that makes all life on Earth possible. Green plants can use the sun's energy to produce food. Many cells in the leaves of green plants contain chlorophyll. Chlorophyll absorbs energy from sunlight. Carbon dioxide and water combine by using the light energy absorbed by chlorophyll to form sugar and oxygen. This process is called photosynthesis. Plants and animals must be able to use the products of photosynthesis (food and oxygen) to produce the energy needed to grow and support life functions.

Respiration is the process of using food and oxygen to produce energy, water, and carbon dioxide. Respiration occurs in the living cells of all living organisms.

The stems of vascular plants have xylem and phloem tissue that transports water, dissolved nutrients, and food throughout the plants. Vascular plants can grow very large because these transport tissues grow as the plants grow and provide all the needed substances to all parts of the growing plants. Nonvascular plants don't have xylem and phloem tissues, therefore they can't grow as large as vascular plants.

Critical Thinking

1. Compare the processes of photosynthesis and respiration in regard to energy.

2. Which would have more stomata, a desert plant or a forest plant? Why?

3. Which layers of cells do roots and stems have in common?

4. Would trees in tropical regions have annual growth rings? Why or why not?

5. Why can't animals use the energy from sunlight to make food?

HOW
Do Plants
Reproduce?

Flowers produce seeds. Pine cones produce seeds. New plants can develop from seeds. Mosses produce spores. New moss plants can develop from spores. Some plants can develop from other plant parts. In this lesson, you'll learn about the different ways that plants reproduce.

Do you have a favorite flower? Is this flower your favorite because of how it looks or because of how it smells or both? Did you buy this flower in a flower shop, did you grow it in a pot or in a garden, or did you see it in a field or alongside a road? Describe your favorite flower to a classmate. Draw a picture of this flower for your classmate and try to describe how it smells.

Flowers give many people enjoyment. People give flowers as gifts to express affection or appreciation. But flowers are also very important to many kinds of plants. Flowers are the reproductive structures for most seed-bearing plants.

Many animals interact with flowers. These animals depend on flowers for food. Flowers and animals have a very interesting relationship. Maybe you've heard the phrase "The birds and the bees, the flowers and the trees…" But what about the bats and the cactus?

Cactus flower in bloom

The flowers of the cardon cactus open only at night. Blooming at night helps this desert plant conserve its limited supply of water. A bat darting silently through the dark night sky smells the cactus flowers as they begin to open. These flowers are white and easy to see, even on a moonless night. The bat swoops down and buries its head in the opening flower. It laps up the sweet nectar inside the flower and eats some of the pollen grains. The bat then flies to another cactus plant with an opening flower to feed again. Some pollen grains from the first flower have stuck to the bat's furry face. These grains are brushed off as the bat buries its head inside the second cactus flower. The pollen grains from the flower of the first cardon cactus plant can come into contact with the reproductive structures of the flowers of the second cardon cactus plant. How does this benefit the cardon cactus species?

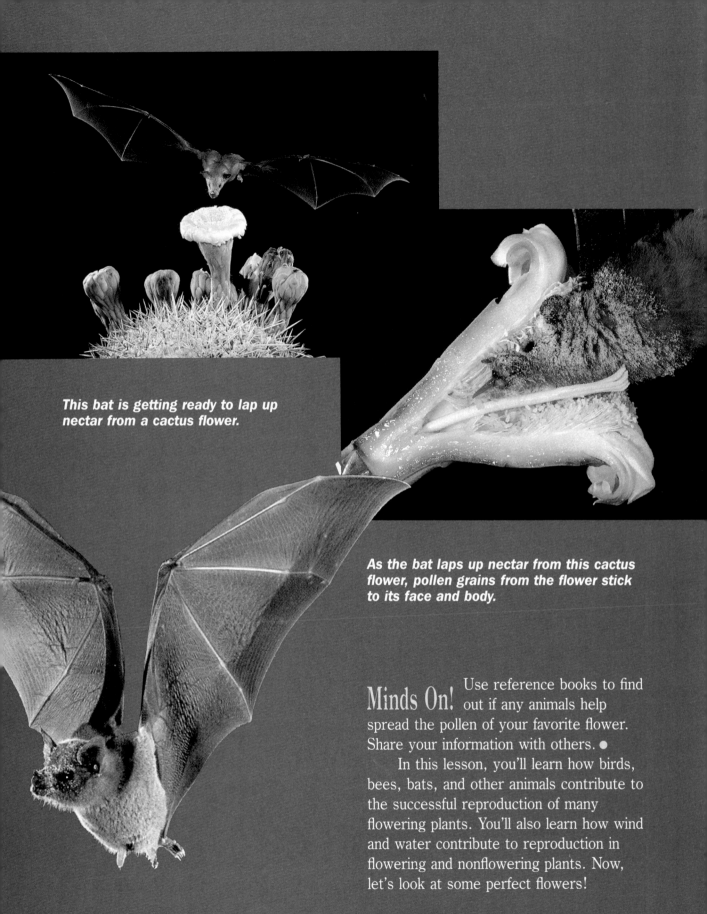

This bat is getting ready to lap up nectar from a cactus flower.

As the bat laps up nectar from this cactus flower, pollen grains from the flower stick to its face and body.

Minds On!
Use reference books to find out if any animals help spread the pollen of your favorite flower. Share your information with others. ●

In this lesson, you'll learn how birds, bees, bats, and other animals contribute to the successful reproduction of many flowering plants. You'll also learn how wind and water contribute to reproduction in flowering and nonflowering plants. Now, let's look at some perfect flowers!

Activity!

What is a Perfect Flower?

Flowers come in many sizes, shapes, colors, and scents. Do all flowers have the same kind and number of flower parts and the same kind of stems and leaves?

What You Need

lily flower, stem, and leaves
gladiolus flower, stem, and leaves
geranium flower, stem, and leaves
petunia flower, stem, and leaves
8 glass slides
8 coverslips
microscope
dropper
plastic cup
water
Activity Log pages 18-19

What To Do

1 Examine each flower with its stem and leaves. Record the name of each flower, along with its color and number of petals, in your *Activity Log*.

2 Each group member should pick one flower to work with for the rest of this activity. Do not remove the stem and leaves from your flower.

3 Examine the reproductive structures inside the petals of your flower. Find the structures called the stamens that contain yellow pollen grains on top. How many stamens are in your flower? Record this number in your *Activity Log*. The pollen grains can be shaken or rubbed off the stamens. Shake a few pollen grains onto a clean glass slide. Add a drop of water and a coverslip. Observe the grains under low power of a microscope. Observe the pollen grains from the flowers of

each of your group members. Sketch the appearance of these grains in your *Activity Log*.

4 Find the reproductive structure inside the petals of your flower that has a sticky area on top. This structure is called the pistil. Shake a few of the pollen grains from a stamen onto this structure. Do they stick? How many pistils are in your flower? Record this number in your *Activity Log*. Have your teacher open a pistil. Remove the contents of the pistil and place one of the pieces, called an ovule, on a clean glass slide. Add a drop of water and a coverslip. Observe the ovule under low power of the microscope. Observe the ovules from the flowers of each of your group members. Sketch the appearance of these ovules in your *Activity Log*.

What Happened?

1. Did the pollen grains from all the flowers in your group look the same under the microscope? Describe the similarities or differences in your *Activity Log*.
2. Did the ovules from the pistils from all the flowers in your group look the same under the microscope? Describe the similarities or differences in your *Activity Log*.
3. Were the pistils more sturdy or more flexible than the stamens? Why do you think this is so?

What Now?

1. With your group, discuss ways that pollen from the stamen can be transferrred to the pistil.
2. In your *Activity Log*, record whether each flower in your group contained both stamens and pistils.
3. Examine the leaves and stems of everyone's flower in your group. Can you see a relationship between the structures of the leaves and stems and the number of petals of each flower? If so, describe this relationship in your *Activity Log*.

Angiosperms—Parts and Reproductive Processes

A perfect flower has both pistil and stamens. An imperfect flower has one or the other. In the Explore Activity, you examined several perfect flowers.

Flowering plants are classified as angiosperms. The word *angiosperm* comes from two Greek words, *angeion* and *sperma*. *Angeion* means "closed container," and *sperma* means "seed." **Angiosperms** (an´ jē ə spûrmz) are vascular plants that produce seeds inside fruits, which form from flowers. Angiosperms consist of a root system and a shoot system. The shoot system is the aboveground part of plants—the stem and leaves. The flowers develop from the shoot system. How do angiosperms produce seeds? First, let's look at the parts of a complete flower.

Pistils are the female reproductive organs of a flower.

The stigma is the sticky top part of the pistil.

A stalk called a style connects the ovary to the stigma.

A pistil consists of an ovary at the base that produces ovules. Ovules are the structures that contain female gametophytes that contain female sex cells.

A complete flower contains sepals, petals, stamens, and pistils.

Sepals are leaflike parts of a flower that protect the flower when it is a young bud.

Stamens are the male reproductive organs of a flower.

Stamens consist of a stalk called a filament.

On top of the filament is a structure called an anther where pollen is formed.

Petals are leaflike and usually brightly colored parts that surround the pistils and stamens. Petals are bright and showy to attract pollinators.

Now that you've seen the parts of a complete flower in the Explore Activity, let's see how and where seeds are produced.

Pollination occurs when pollen grains from the anthers are carried by water, wind, or animals to the stigma. When a pollen grain lands on the sticky stigma, a tube grows downward through the style, into the ovary, and into the ovule. **Fertilization** occurs when a male sex cell from the pollen grain moves down through the pollen tube and fuses with a female sex cell in the ovule. A sex cell is a gamete. Within the ovule, the male gamete and the female gamete join to form a new cell called a zygote. The zygote then develops into an embryo. An embryo is a young growing plant. As the embryo grows, the outer layers of the ovule become tough layers to form a **seed coat.** The seed coat protects the embryo after it is released into the environment. The **seed** consists of the embryo, stored food, and the seed coat. The ovary that surrounds a seed or seeds gets larger and develops into the fruit. A **fruit** is a ripened ovary of a flower that contains one or more seeds.

Seeds are usually carried away from the parent plant. This process is called **seed dispersal.** Fruits assist in seed dispersal, as well as in seed protection.

If a pollen grain lands on a stigma, a pollen tube grows down through the style into the ovary.

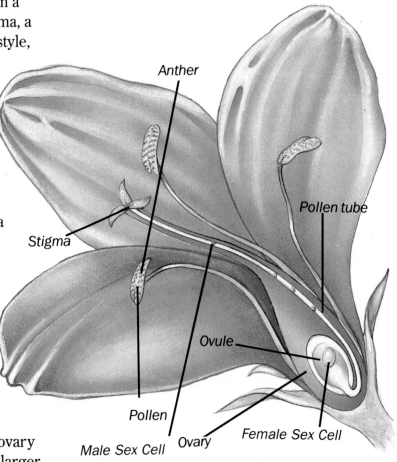

Anther

Pollen tube

Stigma

Ovule

Pollen

Female Sex Cell

Male Sex Cell

Ovary

Minds On! Get together with three other students and brainstorm a list of reasons telling why seed dispersal is important. Hint: Recall from Lesson 1 that roots absorb water and dissolved nutrients, and from Lesson 2 that leaves absorb sunlight for photosynthesis. Share your lists with the rest of your class. ●

Do the Try This Activity on the next page to look at several simple fruits and the seeds within these fruits.

Activity!

From Flowers to Fruits

A simple fruit develops from a single ripened ovary in the pistil of a flower. There are two kinds of simple fruits, dry and fleshy. Some dry fruits split open when they are ripe, others do not. Let's look at several dry and fleshy fruits. As you are examining each fruit, consider how each fruit contributes to seed dispersal and seed protection.

What You Need

fresh pea pod, corn grain, walnut, apple, cherry, tomato, sharp knife, hammer, goggles, *Activity Log* **page 20**

1. Examine a fresh pea pod. Draw and label the pea pod in your *Activity Log*. Is this a dry or a fleshy fruit? Carefully break open the ovary wall and observe how the seeds are fastened. Record the number of seeds in the pea pod in your *Activity Log*. Do the seeds separate easily from the ovary wall?
2. Examine a corn grain. Draw and label the corn grain in your *Activity Log*. Is this a dry or a fleshy fruit? Record the number of seeds in the corn grain in your *Activity Log*. How is this corn grain different from the pea pod?
3. Examine a walnut. Draw and label the walnut in your *Activity Log*. Is this a dry or a fleshy fruit? Record the number of seeds in the walnut in your Activity Log. How is the walnut different from the pod and the grain?

   Grains, pods, and nuts are dry fruits. How do you think the seeds inside dry fruits are dispersed? Think about the size of these fruits and how much they weigh.
4. Cut the apple in half lengthwise. *Safety Tip:* Use the knife carefully and safely. Draw and label the apple half in your *Activity Log*. Is this a dry or a fleshy fruit? In your *Activity Log*, record the number of seeds in your apple half. An apple core is actually the ripened ovary of the flower. Can you see any flower parts on this apple?
5. Cut the cherry lengthwise through the center. Draw and label the cherry half in your *Activity Log*. Is this a dry or a fleshy fruit? Remove the stone. Use a hammer to tap the stone gently until it breaks open. What do you see?
6. Cut a tomato crosswise through the center. Observe the seeds. Draw and label the tomato half in your *Activity Log*. Is this a dry or a fleshy fruit? A tomato is a berry. A berry is a fleshy, enlarged ovary. The seeds are embedded in the flesh, and a thin skin surrounds the fruit. In your *Activity Log*, record the number of seeds in your tomato half. What are some other berries?

   How do you think the seeds inside fleshy fruits are scattered? Think about the people and animals that eat the fruits.

Now that you've learned how and where the seeds of flowering plants are produced and how they are dispersed, let's find out what's inside these seeds.

All seeds are covered by a seed coat and contain an embryo and stored food. The young leaves in the embryo of a seed are called **cotyledons** (kot´ ə lē´ dənz). Monocot (mon´ ə kot´) seed embryos contain one cotyledon. *Mono-* means "one," and *-cot* is part of the word *cotyledon*. In monocot seeds, stored nutrients for the growing embryo are located in the endosperm. The endosperm is the main part of a corn seed you eat. Dicot (dī´ kot) seed embryos contain two cotyledons. *Di-* means "two," and *-cot* is part of the word *cotyledon*. In dicot seeds, stored nutrients for the growing embryo are located in the cotyledons. Cotyledons are the main part of a bean seed you eat.

A corn seed contains one cotyledon.

Remember that an embryo is a young growing plant within a seed. **Germination** is the early growth of a new plant from the embryo in a seed. This young, growing plant needs the stored nutrients in the endosperm or the cotyledons to support its life functions when it germinates. Do the Try This Activity on this page to examine the embryos in a monocot seed and a dicot seed.

Now let's look at the plants that develop from the embryos in monocot seeds and dicot seeds.

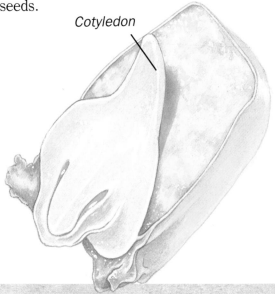
Cotyledon

TRY THIS
Activity!

Examining Embryos

Can you locate the shoot and root of the embryos in a bean seed and a corn seed?

What You Need
soaked bean seeds, soaked corn seeds, hand lens, *Activity Log* page 21

1. Examine a soaked corn seed. On one side you may see a structure that sticks out a little. This is the embryo.

2. Use a hand lens to look at a cut corn seed. Locate the shoot section and the root section of the embryo. Draw and label these in your *Activity Log*.

3. Remove the seed coat of the soaked bean seed. Carefully pull apart the 2 halves of the bean seed. Locate the shoot section and the root section of the embryo. Draw and label these in your *Activity Log*.

4. In your *Activity Log*, compare and contrast the embryos in the corn seed and the bean seed. Record where the stored nutrients in each of these seeds are located. Do you think the plants that develop from these embryos will look alike?

A bean seed contains two cotyledons.

Cotyledons

Monocot flower: Petals and sepals are in multiples of three.
Leaves are narrow and contain parallel veins.

Dicot flower: Petals and sepals are in multiples of four or five. Leaves are broad and contain branched veins.

In plants, the generation that is produced by the germination and growth of a seed is called a sporophyte. The sporophyte contains structures that undergo meiosis to produce spores. Remember that when a cell undergoes meiosis, daughter cells result that have half the number of chromosomes in their nuclei as the original cell.

The spores produced by meiosis develop into the gametophyte generation of the plant. Sex cells are produced as the gametophyte undergoes mitosis. You remember from Lesson 1 that mitosis is cell division that results in two cells with the exact same number of chromosomes as the original cell. Since the cells in the gametophyte have half the number of chromosomes as the sporophyte, mitosis produces sex cells with half the number of chromosomes.

When sex cells formed in the male and female gametophytes join, a new cell results that has the original number of chromosomes. This process is called sexual reproduction. **Sexual reproduction** is the fertilization of a female sex cell by a male sex cell. The new cell that results is the zygote that develops into an embryo inside a seed. A new sporophyte plant will develop from the embryo if the right conditions exist.

Pollination—The Process of Moving Pollen

How does pollination occur? When pollen from the anther of a flower on one plant lands on the stigma of a flower from another plant, **cross-pollination** occurs. A seed that results from cross-pollination will contain hereditary information from two different parent plants. When pollen from a flower on one plant lands on the stigma of the same flower or on the stigma of another flower on the same plant, **self-pollination** occurs. A seed that results from self-pollination contains hereditary information from one parent plant.

The flowers of most plants have characteristics that favor cross-pollination. Some of these are nectar (a sweet, sugary substance), bright colors, and sweet smells. Birds and insects are attracted by the colors, smells, and nectar of many flowers. They pollinate many other flowers on different plants of the same species as they move from plant to plant in search of nectar and pollen. Just as in the story of the bat and cactus at the beginnning of this lesson, some pollen grains stick to the birds and insects that feed on the nectar and pollen. These pollen grains are then moved from flower to flower by the birds and insects. Can people help to pollinate flowers? *1*

As this bird takes nectar from the flower, it brushes against pollen grains which stick to its feathers.

As this drop of water falls from the anther of a flower it carries some pollen grains.

Minds On! Read each situation below and decide whether it describes cross-pollination or self-pollination.

1. A bee sips nectar from a sage flower. The bee brushes against the anthers of this flower. Pollen grains from the anthers rub off onto the bee's wings. The bee flies to another sage plant and feeds on the flowers of this plant. Some of the pollen grains rub off onto the stigmas of the second sage flower.

2. A raindrop lands on a lily flower. It lands on an anther, picks up some pollen grains, and drips off onto the stigma of the same flower.

3. A gust of wind blows some pollen grains of a gladiolus flower onto the stigma of this flower and also onto the stigma of another flower on the same gladiolus plant. ●

This bee covered with pollen can carry pollen to another flower.

Gymnosperms—
Parts and Reproductive
Processes

Not all plants that produce seeds have flower. **Gymnosperms** (jim′ nə spûrmz) are seed-bearing vascular plants that do not produce seeds in flowers and do not have fruits to help in seed dispersal and protection. The word *gymnosperm* comes from the Greek words *gymnos* and *sperma*. *Gymnos* means "naked," and *sperma* means "seed." Plants such as pine trees and spruce trees are gymnosperms. Most gymnosperms are conifers. The leaves of conifers are needle-shaped or scalelike. Most conifers are evergreens. Conifers produce seeds on the woody scales of cones rather than inside the pistils of flowers. Have you ever collected pine cones from the floor of a forest or seen pine cones used in wintertime decorations?

The seeds of conifers aren't produced inside a flower nor enclosed by a fruit. How are they scattered away from the parent plant? Do the Try This Activity below to examine conifer seeds and discover how they are dispersed.

Pine cones cover the floor of this woods.

TRY THIS
Activity!

Winged Seeds

What You Need
two-year-old female pine cone, hand lens, white sheet of paper, *Activity Log* page 22

Draw and label the pine cone in your *Activity Log*. Smell the pine cone. How does it smell? Is it colorful? How do you think pine cones are pollinated?

Look for a scale that has two winged seeds on its upper surface. Use your fingernail or the tip of a pencil to remove the seeds and place them on a white sheet of paper. Examine the seeds with a hand lens, and sketch them in your *Activity Log*. Why do you think these seeds have wings?

Pine trees are typical gymnosperms. Pines produce male and female cones on the mature tree, or sporophyte. The scales that form these cones carry structures called sporangia that produce male and female gametophytes. A gametophyte is the structure in the life cycle of a plant that forms gametes, or sex cells. Female cones consist of a spiral of woody scales on a short stem. Two ovules produce female sex cells on top of each scale. Male cones are smaller and less woody than female cones and are found at the tips of the pine branches in the spring. The male cones produce pollen grains, which contain the male sex cells.

Millions of pollen grains can be released from a male pine cone. After the pollen is released, the male cone falls from the tree. Pollen grains are carried by the wind and eventually may land on a female cone. If the pollen grains land between the scales of a female cone and come into contact with the ovules, a tube grows from the pollen grain into the ovule. A male sex cell from the pollen grain fertilizes the female sex cell in the ovule. A zygote is formed and develops into a tiny embryo

inside the ovule. This ovule with the embryo becomes the pine seed. During the fall and winter, female cones fall off the pine trees. The scales spread open, and the seeds fall out and can be carried or blown away. If the seeds land where conditions are right for germination, a new pine tree will grow.

Now let's look at the life cycle of a moss to see how nonvascular plants reproduce. Male sex cells are formed in male sex organs at the tops of leafy moss stems called gametophytes. Female sex cells are formed in the tips of female gametophytes. Male sex cells are splashed by water onto female gametophytes and swim to the female sex cells. When a male and a female sex cell join, a zygote is formed. This part of the life cycle is due to sexual reproduction. The zygote develops into a long, thin stalk from the tip of the female gametophyte. A capsule forms at the top of this stalk. Spores are formed inside the capsule. The capsule and stalk are the sporophyte. The capsule bursts, and the spores are forced out. If spores land on a moist surface, they will develop into a moss plant.

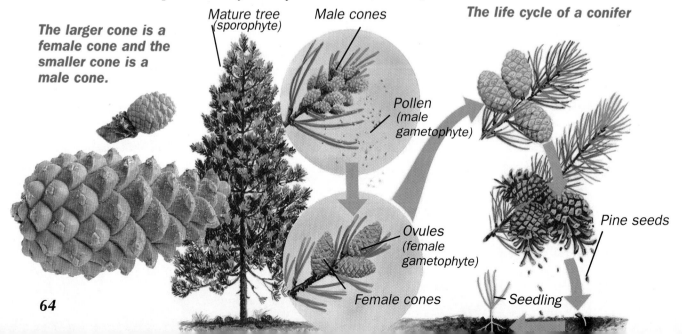

The larger cone is a female cone and the smaller cone is a male cone.

Mature tree (sporophyte)

Male cones

The life cycle of a conifer

Pollen (male gametophyte)

Ovules (female gametophyte)

Female cones

Pine seeds

Seedling

A fern is a vascular plant that reproduces by using spores.

In seed-bearing plants, the female gametophyte is contained in an ovule and the male gametophyte is contained in a pollen grain. The sporophyte in seed-bearing plants is the new plant that grows from the embryo.

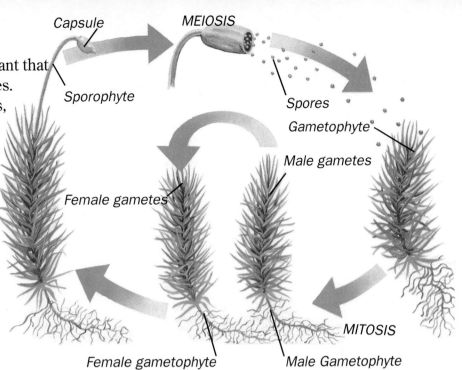

The life cycle of a moss

Minds On!

Work with another student to compare and contrast the life cycle of a moss with the life cycle of an angiosperm. Are spores formed by angiosperms? Do mosses form seeds? Answer these questions and write any other similarities and differences you can think of on *Activity Log* page 23. •

You've learned that angiosperms, gymnosperms, and mosses undergo sexual reproduction. Are there any other ways that plants can reproduce?

Can a new plant be grown from a structure other than a seed or a spore? Plants can reproduce by asexual reproduction. **Asexual reproduction** is reproduction by any process that does not involve gametes (male and female sex cells). Vegetative propagation (vej′ i tā′ tiv prop′ ə gā′ shən) is a type of asexual reproduction. A new plant can be grown from parts (other than seeds or spores) of other plants by vegetative propagation. Gametes are not involved. During vegetative propagation, growth occurs by the process of mitosis. Do the Try This Activity on this page to see the results of vegetative propagation.

TRY THIS Activity!

Starting New Plants Without Seeds

You can see the results of vegetative propagation in a Kalanchoe plant leaf or an African violet plant leaf.

What You Need
small milk carton, sand, leaf from Kalanchoe or African violet plant, water, *Activity Log* page 24

Fill the milk carton with sand and add a small amount of water to the sand. Obtain a leaf from a Kalanchoe plant or an African violet plant. Place the leaf on the sand. Add a small amount of sand on top of the stem end of the leaf. Check the leaf every day. In your ***Activity Log***, make a drawing of the leaf every week. What formed along the edges of the leaf?

65

Why Don't Roses Bloom in the Snow?

You've learned that flowers are the reproductive structures in which most seeds are produced. Why do flowers appear and bloom when they do? Many flowering plants won't produce flowers until they're a certain age or size. Then they must receive the proper environmental signals. Some of these environmental signals include temperature, day length, and availability of nutrients. **Photoperiodism** (fō´ tō pîr´ ē əd iz əm) is the response of the plant to flower based on the length of the day. Long-day plants flower when the days are longer during spring and summer. Short-day plants flower when the days are shorter during late summer and autumn. How could short-day plants be made to flower during spring and summer? A floriculturist (flôr´ i kul chər ist) would need to know how to do this.

CAREERS

Floriculturist

Floriculturists practice floriculture. Floriculture is the science, art, and business of growing decorative plants. Many decorative plants are flowering plants. In warm climates, these flowering plants can be grown outside. In cold climates, flowering plants are grown in heated greenhouses.

Floriculturists can control the blooming of flowers. They can do this by regulating the temperature and amount of sunlight that plants receive. A floriculturist might force short-day plants such as chrysanthemums to bloom in spring or summer by shielding the plants during the mornings and evenings with black cloth or black paper. This reduces the number of hours of sunlight they receive. Long-day plants can be forced to bloom in winter in greenhouses by artificially increasing the amount of light that these plants receive.

Floriculturists work in florist shops, plant nurseries, private gardens, or zoos.

The Nature Book

"Like animals, many flowers sleep at a fixed time. When they're asleep the flowers close or hang down. Next day they're wide open again. Select some plants and keep a log of what time their flowers open and close. . . .

Some flowers are so punctual that you can use them to make a clock. Each of the twelve digits on the clock face will be a different kind of flower, opening or closing or smelling most sweetly at the hour it represents."

In Midas Dekkers' reference handbook, *The Nature Book,* flowers are part of a flowerclock. Of course flowers don't really sleep, but they do open and close at certain times. Find flowering plants in your area that have specific times to open, close, or smell sweetest. Design a clock face using your flower timers.

Flowers are often the subject of many paintings and photographs. Mary Wolcott was an artist who became famous for her watercolor paintings of wild flowers. In 1925, the Smithsonian Institute published five volumes of her North American Wild flowers. Her paintings are admired for their beauty and accuracy.

Once flowers have bloomed and have produced seeds, what causes the seeds to germinate? As a seed completes its development and is ready to be dispersed, it becomes very dry. Germination begins with the uptake of water by the dry seed. If the temperature is favorable for growth, the seed will germinate. Some seeds require cold temperatures for germination, and some seeds require warm temperatures.

The seeds of plants that grow in climates that have four seasons often need a period of exposure to freezing temperatures. This ensures that these seeds will germinate only in spring and will have a whole growing season ahead.

Germinating seed

A **dormant seed** has not germinated but still has the potential to germinate. How long can seeds remain dormant? This varies from plant to plant. Some seeds thought to be 10,000 years old have germinated. Other seeds are able to germinate for only a few weeks.

Is there any way to save seeds from plants that may be in danger of extinction?

Focus on Technology
Saving Seeds

Prehistoric farmers began saving seeds more than twenty thousand years ago. They stored seeds in cool, dry places—often in clay pots that protected the seeds from insects and mice. Keeping seeds dormant enabled these early farmers to grow crops of the same kinds of food year after year.

Scientists are now using new techniques for storing seeds of rare plants. Some of these plants may be used for making medicines in the future. Others may be used to make crops resistant to drought or plant diseases. The seeds of many crop plants can be stored quite easily for years— perhaps even hundreds of years—by freezing them in liquid nitrogen at −196°C.

This tray of seeds will be placed in water-proof bags and placed into storage at very low temperatures.

Many potentially useful plants are in danger of becoming extinct because of widespread clearing and burning of the rain forests. Freezing the seeds of these plants is not a good way to preserve them. However, scientists have discovered that the seeds of rain forest plants can be preserved by storing them in nitrous oxide gas. A seed stored in nitrous oxide gas slows its respiration to half the normal rate. This allows the period of dormancy to be longer. The seeds resume their regular respiration rate when exposed to normal air again and can then germinate.

Sum It Up

The reproductive structures in flowers interact to produce seeds. In the Explore Activity, you examined several perfect flowers. Perfect flowers have both male and female reproducutive structures. Imperfect flowers have either male or female structures. Female reproductive structures contain female sex cells, and male reproductive structures contain male sex cells. The movement of male sex cells to female reproductive structures is called pollination. Birds and insects pollinate flowering plants. After flowers are pollinated, a male sex cell joins with a female sex cell to form a zygote. Zygotes develop into an embryo inside a seed. Seeds germinate and develop into new plants.

The reproductive structures in pine cones also interact to produce seeds that can germinate and grow into new pine trees. Wind pollinates pine cones.

Mosses reproduce by producing female sex cells and male sex cells, which combine to form a sporophyte. The sporophyte produces spores which can develop into a new moss plant. Mosses require water for transfer of the male sex cell to the female sex cell.

Environmental signals affect the blooming of flowers.

Seeds can be saved by freezing or exposure to nitrous oxide.

Critical Thinking

1. Why do mosses need to grow in moist places to reproduce sexually?
2. How are seeds an adaptation to living on land?
3. Why are some flowers brightly colored?
4. Can an imperfect flower pollinate itself? Explain.
5. What could cause a dormant seed to germinate?

How Do Plants Respond to the Environment?

Most plants spend their lives in one location. They are anchored to this location by their roots. But to survive, plants must be able to respond to various environmental conditions. How do plants respond to environmental conditions over time? The answer has to do with evolution. It involves the stability of the whole species, not just of the plant in danger.

In the summer of 1988, Yellowstone National Park burned. High winds and lower-than-average rainfall had made the trees and bushes drier than firewood. Lightning soon turned Yellowstone into a patchwork of giant bonfires.

Most of the animal life in the park escaped unharmed. A few elk and bison (buffalo) died in the fires, but far fewer than a hard winter kills. Birds and insects flew to safe areas. Small animals ran away from the flames or took cover in burrows as the fires passed over. People visiting the park all left safely, sometimes driving convoys of cars through blinding clouds of smoke. Just one fire fighter was killed by a falling tree. But what about the plant life?

Fire moving through grassy meadows burned the driest parts of small plants. By the following spring, the meadows showed little evidence of having been burned.

In other areas, the fire burned along the forest floor. It consumed dead wood, fallen leaves, and underbrush. The living trees were scorched, but most survived. September rains and an early snowfall finally put out these blazes.

In the hardest-hit areas, the fire left only bare ground. The heat of the flames even shattered boulders. Ashes and a few smouldering stumps of trees that once towered 30 meters (about 100 feet) were all that remained of an old-growth forest. How and when would these plants be replaced?

Plants respond to changes in light, water, or attacks by insects more often than they face destruction in a large-scale disaster. Forest fires are spectacular events that can suddenly change plant living conditions in an area. However, most of the environmental changes that affect plants take longer to develop, or they occur on a much smaller scale.

This venus flytrap plant grows in nitrogen-poor soil. It can capture flies and use the nitrogen in their bodies for nutrients.

Minds On! Here are some examples of small-scale environmental changes that could affect a plant or group of plants. Discuss each situation with your classmates. Decide how plants might respond to the new conditions. How might the kinds of plants living in these conditions change over many generations?

1. A potted plant raised in an evenly lighted greenhouse is purchased and placed on a windowsill in an apartment. Now only half of its leaves receive direct sunlight. Is there a way that the plant can capture more sunlight for photosynthesis?

2. Rain falls in some desert areas only once or twice a year. When it rains, desert plants need to absorb and store as much water as possible. How might they do this? Since the plants in a dry area store water, how are they protected from being used as a water source by animals or other plants? ●

Desert plants such as this cactus need to absorb and store as much water as possible.

Activity!

How Do Roots and Shoots Know Where To Grow?

When farmers sow seeds in a field, the seeds can land on the ground in almost any position. The shoot of the embryo inside the seed may be pointed up toward the sun or down toward Earth. The root of the embryo may also be pointed up toward the sun or down toward Earth. Can the roots and shoots in plant embryos respond to gravity so that the roots will grow down toward Earth and the shoots will grow up toward the sun?

What You Need

8 lima beans (soaked in water overnight)
self-sealing plastic bag
piece of corrugated cardboard
scissors
several paper towels
water
labels
markers
tape
Activity Log pages 25-26

What To Do

1 In your group, share responsibility to complete the following setup. Cut a piece of cardboard so that it will barely slide inside the plastic bag. Use 2 layers of cardboard if necessary to get a tight fit. Remove the cardboard from the bag and wrap a layer of paper towels around it. Slide the towel-covered cardboard back into the bag. Pour in enough water to soak the cardboard and the towels. Pour off any excess water after the cardboard is thoroughly wet.

2 Slide 8 lima beans inside the bag on top of the towel-covered cardboard. Place the lima beans in a circle.

3 Put your group's names and the date on the bag. Seal the bag. The plastic should stretch snugly over the lima beans and hold them in place. If any of the beans slip out of position, push on the outside of the bag and line them up again. If all of the beans slip, add more cardboard or more paper towels to the bag until you get a tighter fit.

4 Hang the bag in a dark place. Do not lay the bag down flat. Observe the lima beans once a day for the next 3–5 days. In your *Activity Log*, sketch the positions of the roots and the shoots when the seeds sprout. Hang the bag back in the same direction in the dark place after you make your observations.

What Happened?

1. What direction were the roots of the lima beans inside the plastic bag growing on day 1?
2. What direction were the roots growing at the end of day 5?
3. Did some of the roots grow in a curve, or did they all grow straight out of the seeds?
4. Did the shoots of the lima beans all grow straight out of the beans, or did some of them curve? In what direction did the shoots finally point?

What Now?

1. Design an experiment to find out if after day 5, the direction in which the roots and shoots are growing can be made to change.
2. What do you think would happen if a seedling was not able to grow its root down into the soil and its shoot up into the sunlight?

EXPLORE

How Do Plants Survive in Earth's Different Environments?

Plants thrive in seas, deserts, jungles, and in almost every other environment found on Earth. The soil, water, nutrients, amount of sunlight, and temperatures are different in each of these places. Plants can survive on Earth because of adaptations they have developed to respond to different types of environments.

Adaptation is the term used to describe a trait that helps an organism survive in a particular environment. The better adapted an organism is to its environment, the more likely it is to complete its life cycle.

In order to complete their life cycles, living things must obtain a reliable source of nutrients and energy, and they must reproduce. All living organisms have many adaptations that help them complete these tasks. In addition, most organisms have a number of unique adaptations for self-defense. In this lesson, you'll learn about some of the specific adaptations that help plants live on Earth.

Underwater kelp grows toward the light.

Plants in a forest grow toward the light.

Dandelion seeds are dispersed by the wind.

What Is a Plant Behavior?

Plants need sunlight, water, carbon dioxide, oxygen, and dissolved nutrients from the soil in order to survive. When seeds sprout, they must get their roots anchored in the soil and their leaves up into the sunlight. But the first root pushing out of a sprouting seed may be pointing in any direction. If it grows up into the air, the seedling will probably die.

This potted plant grows toward the sunlight.

These desert plants are adapted to a dry environment.

In the Explore Activity, you saw how the root in a growing plant embryo grows downward and how the shoot grows upward. Gravity provides the plant root with a clue about where it will find soil. Gravity is a stimulus to which the plant responds. A **stimulus** (stim´ yə ləs) is something outside a plant in its environment that affects a plant's behavior. A **plant behavior** is the response of a plant to a stimulus. The response of plants to gravity is called gravitropism. If a root is growing horizontally, it will curve downward because the cells on the lower side of the root don't become as long as the cells on the upper side of the root. As the upper cells become longer, the root curves and pushes down into the soil.

Most plants spend their lives anchored in one place by their roots. But a plant can change its position slightly by growing toward or away from a stimulus. This type of plant response is called a **tropism.** Gravitropism is just one example of a tropism. Plants also respond to sunlight (phototropism), to water (hydrotropism), and to touch (thigmotropism). All these tropisms are responses that help the plant survive by obtaining more sunlight, water, or dissolved nutrients from the soil. Do the Try This Activity on the next page to see how plants respond to sunlight.

Activity!

Where's the Light?

How do plants respond to light? Find out.

What You Need

4 soaked lima beans, milk carton, moist sand, shoe box and lid, *Activity Log* page 27

1. Plant 4 soaked lima beans in the moist sand. Plant each bean about 1 cm deep. Place the milk carton inside the shoe box and cover it. Place the box in a warm place. If the sand starts to dry out, add enough water to keep it moist.

2. In 3–7 days, the shoots of the lima beans will sprout. In your *Activity Log*, draw the shoots. When the shoots are 2 or 3 cm (about 1 in.) tall, your teacher will cut a 1-in. opening in the box. Place the box so that the opening faces a strong light source.

3. Observe the seedlings 2 hours after they are exposed to light. Sketch the seedlings in your *Activity Log*. Put the box back so that the opening faces the strong light. Observe the seedlings again the next day and sketch them in your *Activity Log*. How has the light affected them?

Reproductive Adaptations

Plants live longer than any other type of organism on Earth. Bristlecone pine trees over 5,000 years old grow in the southwestern United States. Trees 200 to 500 years old can be found almost anywhere in the U.S. But no plant lives forever. Plants must reproduce or become extinct.

Recall that many plants can undergo vegetative reproduction, as well as producing seeds or spores for reproduction. This adaptation increases the chances that some of the plant's offspring will survive.

Other plants, such as lodgepole pine trees, produce two kinds of seeds. Some of the lodgepole pine's seeds are released every year. These seeds will sprout if they land on fertile soil and other conditions for growth are favorable. The second kind of lodgepole pine seed is held in tightly closed cones as a sort of "life insurance policy"

against fire. These cones won't release seeds unless they've been exposed to the heat of a fire. This adaptation allowed lodgepole seedlings to carpet the soil in areas of Yellowstone National Park where every living tree burned to the ground.

Biologists studying the burned areas of Yellowstone National Park found the ground covered with lodgepole seeds soon after the fires. Each acre of the burned area could have had about 5,800 new trees growing on it if only 1 out of 10 of the seeds sprouted. This is many more trees than an acre of ground could support.

A lodgepole pine cone releases seeds after being burned.

After a forest fire, new green growth occurs.

Plant Adaptations for Dealing With Water Shortages

Desert plants burst into bloom when it rains. Desert plants producing flowers and seeds need more water than is available to them for most of the year. When water is available, many desert plants bloom immediately. The flowers produce drought-resistant seeds that germinate the next time water is available.

Some deserts may not receive rain for several years in a row. Plants that live in deserts must survive on less than 25 centimeters (about 10 inches) of water per year. In order to survive these harsh conditions, desert plants have a variety of adaptations for collecting, storing, and conserving water.

Cactus flowers produce drought-resistant seeds.

Cactus is a common desert plant. Cacti have a thick, waxy covering that reduces the amount of water they lose through their cell walls. The water lost by cactus plants through transpiration is reduced because cactus plants open their stomata only at night.

Cactus roots absorb rainwater very quickly before it evaporates or sinks into the sandy desert soil. Many cactus plants have a pulpy center that swells to absorb water taken up by the roots and shrinks as the water is used up. Cactus spines discourage animals from eating the moist parts of the plant.

Cactus spines discourage people and animals from touching them.

Adaptations That Help Plants Compete With Other Plants

Plants constantly compete with other plants for light, water, and nutrients from the soil. Any plant that is more efficient than neighboring plants in obtaining these necessities of life is likely to survive and reproduce. Plants have developed a vast number of adaptations that help them win this competition for nutrients.

Kudzu is a fast-growing climbing vine. It is considered a weed by some people because it spreads rapidly and is difficult to control. Is kudzu successful at competing for water and nutrients?

Huge quantities of sunlight strike Earth every second. Plants compete to trap a small share of this light. Vines like ivy, wild grapes, and honeysuckle climb trees to capture sunlight. Climbing plants may support themselves by wrapping around the taller plant (thigmotropism), or they may have special sticky structures that attach to the bark of the tree.

Growing tall stems and producing a thick covering of leaves are other adaptations that help plants compete for sunlight and nutrients. Oaks, maples, and other trees grow tall and form a dense canopy of leaves above forests. Their leaves capture most sunlight before it reaches the ground. Other plants have difficulty growing in the dark, shady areas around these trees. Since few large plants can grow close to them, tall trees face less competition for water and nutrients in the soil.

Plant Adaptations That Harm Other Organisms

Have you ever pricked yourself on a thorny plant or developed an itchy skin rash after walking through a patch of weeds near a creek? If you have, you probably try to stay away from these plants now. Thorns and irritating chemicals are examples of plant adaptations.

Plants cannot run away from animals that might harm them. They cannot avoid contact with other plants that may reduce the amount of sunlight and nutrients available to them. Since plants cannot move from dangers, some plants have developed defense mechanisms.

Some plants use chemicals in their competition with other plants. Creosote bushes grow in dry areas of the United States. They release toxic chemicals from their roots into the soil. These chemicals reduce the number of plants growing close to them. This prevents seeds from germinating and may even kill nearby plants. Creosote bushes have less competition for the small amount of water and dissolved nutrients in the soil when they do not grow close to one another.

Stinging nettles contain a watery juice that causes an intense itch when it enters a person's skin.

Poison ivy contains a poisonous oil that is irritating to a person's skin.

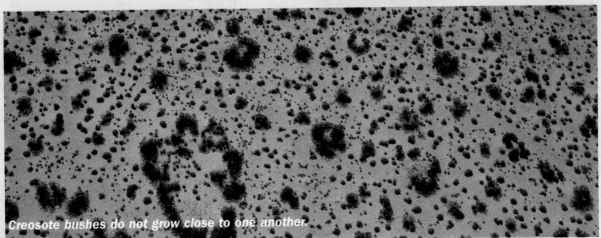

Creosote bushes do not grow close to one another.

Many plants produce poisons that can kill or sicken people that come in contact with the plant. Touching poison ivy causes skin rashes; eating certain holly berries causes vomiting; chewing a stem of hemlock can kill an adult. The best rule for dealing with plants is: never eat or chew any wild plant.

Defensive plant adaptations can be dangerous to humans. But some of the chemicals plants produce to ward off competition are used to produce medicines that ease human suffering and cure serious illnesses.

Over 200 years ago, doctors prepared medicines from the bark of willow trees. The bark contains a chemical that can ease pain and reduce fevers. Scientists later discovered that willow bark contains salicylate—the active ingredient in aspirin. Americans now consume 16,000 tons of aspirin tablets each year—about 80 million pills.

Periwinkle plant

Vincristine is a potent anti-cancer drug used to treat leukemia (cancer of the blood-producing system). It is made from periwinkle plants that grow in Madagascar. Vincristine is poisonous and expensive to produce. However, in controlled dosages, its toxic effects can be counteracted. It has saved the lives of thousands of people.

Willow tree

Willow bark and aspirin

Focus on Technology

Genetic Engineering in Plants

Genetic engineering may soon allow scientists to transfer the genes for useful adaptations from plant to plant. This process has already been shown to work in tobacco and tomato plants. Researchers are working to produce seeds for crops that will resist plant diseases, have high food values, and produce their own insecticides for fighting off plant pests.

Here is an example of how genetic engineering works. A gene is a small part of the material inside the nucleus of a cell. Genes contain the instructions that a cell uses to assemble all the substances the cell makes. The first task of genetic engineers is to find the gene for a useful adaptation, such as resistance to a disease. For example, scientists are currently searching for a gene that will help prevent leaf rust.

Plant laboratory

Leaf rust is a disease that damages corn crops. Scientists know that some plants produce a substance that enables them to fight off this infection. Finding the gene for this adaptation is not easy. Every plant being tested has about twenty thousand genes. Only one plant in 100,000 contains the gene for resistance to leaf rust.

If scientists can locate and isolate the gene for leaf rust resistance, they will then try to transfer this gene into varieties of corn that are grown commercially. The potential value of producing new disease-resistant plants is great. But so far, scientists have not been able to discover a practical way to transfer genes for disease resistance into corn.

Leaf rust on Indian strawberry leaves

Problems Caused by Imported Plants

Environmental scientists are keenly aware that plants imported from different parts of the world may become serious nuisances in their new environment. Plants grown for food or for decoration in one part of the world may become hard to control in a different location.

South American water hyacinths are beautiful plants. About 100 years ago, some were brought as gifts to people in the United States. The offspring of these water hyacinths have become the most damaging water plant in North America.

Water hyacinths are a problem because of their incredibly high rate of reproduction. Scientists in Louisiana reported that in one growing season, 25 of these plants could produce approximately two million offspring. That's enough water hyacinths to form a dense mat completely covering a pond about the size of two football fields. This mass of plant material weighs about as much as a fully loaded jumbo jet.

Water hyacinths don't directly affect food crops, but they still harm human beings. Mats of water hyacinths prevent boats from going through canals, interfering with trade. They clog irrigation ditches and water pipes. Water hyacinths also use up the oxygen in the water, driving off or killing fish.

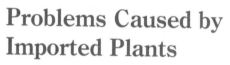

Water hyacinths

No Western movie is complete without a picture of a tumbleweed blowing across the range or rolling down the street of a deserted town. Tumbleweed is more common than ten-gallon hats. But this "Western" plant is actually a form of thistle imported into the United States by accident from Russia around 1877.

Tumbleweed was becoming a problem plant in some western states by the 1890s, causing sharp losses of wheat production. In addition to damaging crops, tumbleweeds' sharp spines can injure horses and cattle. In the fall when its seeds are ripe, its roots break off. It tumbles for miles across open land spreading its seeds as it bounces along. Tumbleweed was not brought under control until new herbicides were invented during the 1940s. Killing tumbleweed is still a major expense for farmers and ranchers.

Sum It Up

Plant adaptations ensure that new generations of plants fit into their environments more successfully. The stability of the species is maintained when plants respond to harsh conditions and thrive rather than die. Plant adaptations include forming thorns and poison to defend a plant against animal attack, growing long stems and broad leaves to reach the sunlight, sending out many seeds to ensure the survival of some of them, and many more. As plants have evolved over millions of years, they have adapted to many changing environments. The constant change has resulted in many thousands of varieties of plants, each with its own particular genetic inheritance that has adapted it to succeed.

Critical Thinking

1. Would the roots of a seedling grow downward in outer space? Why or why not?
2. How could asexual reproduction help a plant survive a forest fire?
3. Why must seedless grapes be reproduced by vegetative reproduction?
4. Insect-eating plants such as pitcher plants and sundews grow in areas where there is little nitrogen in the soil. How are these plants adapted to get the nitrogen they need?
5. Suppose you find a tree on which three different kinds of apples are growing. How could this plant have been developed?

Tumbleweed

F R O M
Acorn to Oak Tree
A Life Story

Germinating acorns

In upper New York state during October, a small squirrel gathering food for the winter found several acorns beneath a white oak tree. One by one, the squirrel buried these acorns in the soil far away from the oak tree. The squirrel planned to return to get them when needed. However, the squirrel did not return to get one of the acorns. The next spring, something happened.

Spring rains provided the soil with plenty of water. Some water moved into the acorn, and the acorn swelled. Its seed coat split open. The acorn contained an embryo and stored food. When the seed coat split open, the embryo began to grow rapidly.

The primary root grew downward from the seed. A root cap on the primary root protected the new root as it pushed its way through the soil. A region behind the root cap contained cells that began dividing rapidly. These rapidly dividing cells became different tissues—the cambium, xylem, phloem, cortex, and epidermis.

Young white oak tree

As the root began to absorb water and dissolved nutrients from the soil, the shoot system began to move upward toward the sun. The stem consisted of the same tissues as the root system. Leaves developed from the stems. The xylem and phloem from the roots were continuous through the stems and into the leaves. Water and dissolved nutrients absorbed by the roots from the soil moved through the stems and into the leaves. The epidermis of the leaves contained stomata through which carbon dioxide gas could diffuse into the leaves. Some of the cells of the leaves contained chlorophyll. The chlorophyll captured sunlight and helped convert carbon dioxide and water into food. This food moved through the phloem tissues to the other parts of the seedling that needed the food for growth.

As the oak-tree seedling continued to make food and grow, the root and shoot systems continued to develop. The root system became very large as it snaked its way through the soil. The shoot system became larger and larger as more and more leaves made food for the tree's growth. The trunk of the tree increased in size around and upward.

White oaks are deciduous trees. Since this one grew in upstate New York, it experienced four seasons each year. During spring and summer, growth occurred. During autumn and winter, leaves dropped off and the tree's growth slowed down.

Soon 20 years had passed. The next spring, the oak tree produced male flowers and female flowers. Wind carried pollen from a male flower to a female flower. A male sex cell from a pollen grain on the male flower fertilized a female sex cell in the ovary of the female flower. A seed developed. The ovary, which contained the seed, developed into an acorn, the fruit of the oak tree. This acorn dropped from the oak tree and was picked up by a squirrel. What do you think happened next?

Did you realize that you knew so much about plants? Now that you've studied them from seed to maturity, you're ready to put your knowledge of plants to work. Tell a life story of the growth of a seed in the Try This Activity below.

White oak tree flowers

Activity!

A Life Story

Choose a plant from the seed-bearing plants listed below. Research this plant and its environment. Write the story of this plant from the germination of its seed to the production of seeds as an adult plant.

Decide how to present your story to your class. You could illustrate your story and post it on the bulletin board, you could read the story aloud, or you could perform a dance that tells the story. Or perhaps several of you who choose plants from the same environment will choose to write a skit and act it out.

Tropical Rain Forest—palm trees, orchids, cinchona trees, bird-of-paradise plants, African violets

Temperate Deciduous Forest—perennial wildflowers, hickory trees, maple trees, oak trees, birch trees

Grasslands—perennial wildflowers, grasses

Desert—cactus, sagebrush, creosote bushes, desert lilies, desert bluebells

Taiga—pine trees, fir trees, spruce trees

The Effects of Changing Plant Populations

The life stories of plants you and your classmates wrote may all have had happy endings in which your plant successfully reproduced. But in the real world, many plants aren't so lucky. As human populations increase, native plant populations decrease. Scientists are constantly researching ways to produce more food, lumber, and other products from plants. The increasing human population has created the need to clear more and more land of its native plants to harvest lumber and to raise food crops. This loss of native plant populations presents the entire world with serious short-term and long-term problems.

Native plants are cleared to make way for food crops.

The expansion of deserts due to overgrazing is also a worsening problem. In northern Africa, for example, herders have raised goats in dry areas around the Sahara desert for centuries. But as human populations have increased, less and less open land is available for grazing. Starving goats have eaten not only the leaves but even the bark and small branches of trees. Because of this overgrazing, most of the plants in traditional grazing areas have died. At the same time, the herders have cut down most of the other trees in the grazing areas to use for firewood. With few plants left to hold the dry soil in place, large areas of land are turning into deserts. They can no longer support either humans or goats.

Shortages of wood to use as cooking fuel are also becoming a worldwide problem. Nepal is a mountainous country between India and China. The government of Nepal is so concerned about people cutting down forests for firewood that they have assigned army troops and police to protect the remaining trees. The roots of trees help slow the water running down the steep hillsides and hold the soil in place. If the trees are cut down, there is a much greater danger of floods and landslides.

Areas that get plenty of rainfall have other problems with changing plant populations. In areas of South America and Asia, one response to rapidly growing human populations is to clear huge tracts of rain forests. Some of the cleared land is used to grow food crops. Other areas of cleared rain forest are used to produce cattle and crops to export.

The overgrazing of sheep and goats can cause desert land to expand.

Nepalese wood cutters.

Replanting the rain forest

Focus on Environment

Rain Forests—Live or Let Die?

Cutting down rain forests puts thousands of species of plants and animals in danger of becoming extinct. Rain forests are the home of half the plant and animal species living on Earth. Many people who live in or near rain forests need this land to grow food crops or to use for ranching. Many other people think this land shouldn't be used for any reason. They think it should be left alone. What do you think? Get together with several people in your class who have different opinions about this issue. Debate in your group whether rain-forest land should be used for various purposes or left alone so that the diversity of plant and animal species will remain. Or perhaps your group can work out a compromise that would answer both needs.

GLOSSARY

Use the pronunciation key below to help you decode, or read, the pronunciations.

Pronunciation Key

a	at, bad	d	dear, soda, bad
ā	ape, pain, day, break	f	five, defend, leaf, off, cough, elephant
ä	father, car, heart	g	game, ago, fog, egg
âr	care, pair, bear, their, where	h	hat, ahead
e	end, pet, said, heaven, friend	hw	white, whether, which
ē	equal, me, feet, team, piece, key	j	joke, enjoy, gem, page, edge
i	it, big, English, hymn	k	kite, bakery, seek, tack, cat
ī	ice, fine, lie, my	l	lid, sailor, feel, ball, allow
îr	ear, deer, here, pierce	m	man, family, dream
o	odd, hot, watch	n	not, final, pan, knife
ō	old, oat, toe, low	ng	long, singer, pink
ô	coffee, all, taught, law, fought	p	pail, repair, soap, happy
ôr	order, fork, horse, story, pour	r	ride, parent, wear, more, marry
oi	oil, toy	s	sit, aside, pets, cent, pass
ou	out, now	sh	shoe, washer, fish mission, nation
u	up, mud, love, double	t	tag, pretend, fat, button, dressed
ū	use, mule, cue, feud, few	th	thin, panther, both
ü	rule, true, food	th	this, mother, smooth
ù	put, wood, should	v	very, favor, wave
ûr	burn, hurry, term, bird, word, courage	w	wet, weather, reward
ə	about, taken, pencil, lemon, circus	y	yes, onion
b	bat, above, job	z	zoo, lazy, jazz, rose, dogs, houses
ch	chin, such, match	zh	vision, treasure, seizure

active transport: an energy-requiring process in which a substance can move through a cell membrane from an area of low concentration of that substance to an area of high concentration of that substance.

adaptation (ad´ əp tā´ shən): a trait that increases the ability of an organism to survive in its environment.

aerial root (âr´ ē əl rüt): a root that grows above ground from the stem of a plant.

angiosperm (an´ jē ə spûrm´): a seed-bearing plant that produces seeds inside a fruit; flowering plant.

annual plant: a plant that grows, reproduces, and dies within one growing season.

apical meristem (ā´ pi kəl mer´ ə stem): a mass of cells at the tip of a root and shoot that divide and cause growth of the root or shoot.

asexual reproduction (ā sek´ shü əl rē´ prə duk´ shən): the production of offspring from only one parent cell.

biennial plant (bī en´ ē əl plant): a plant that produces leaves and food in one year, and reproduces and dies in the second year.

cambium (kam´ bē əm): a growth tissue that gives rise to new xylem and phloem cells.

chlorophyll (klôr´ ə fil´): a pigment that causes a plant to appear green. Chlorophyll absorbs visible light from the sun to provide the energy for photosynthesis.

chloroplast (klôr´ ə plast´): a disk-like structure in plant cells that contains chlorophyll.

cortex (kôr´ teks): root cells that store food.

cotyledons (kot´ ə lē´ dən): the seed leaves in the embryo of a seed.

cross-pollination (krôs´ pol´ ə nā´ shən): pollination between two plants.

cuticle (kū´ ti kəl): a waxy layer that covers the epidermis of some leaves and reduces water loss.

deciduous tree (di sij´ ü əs trē): a tree that loses all its leaves at the end of each growing season.

diffusion (di fū′ zhən):   the movement of particles from areas where they are more concentrated to where they are less concentrated.

dormancy (dôr′ mən sē):   a period of time when the plant embryo is in a resting stage.

dormant seed: a seed that has not yet germinated but still has the potential to germinate.

epidermis (ep′ i dûr′ mis):   the surface layer of a leaf that protects the inner parts of the leaf.

evergreen tree: a tree that loses its leaves gradually. It never is completely without leaves; therefore it appears ever green.

fertilization (fûr′ tə l ə zā′ shən):   the process in which a male gamete and a female gamete combine to form a zygote.

fibrous roots (fī′ brəs rütz):   clusters of roots that are made up of many small, branching roots that grow near the top level of soil.

fruit (früt):   the ripened ovary of a flower that contains one or more seeds.

germination (jûr′ mə nā′ shən):   the early growth of a plant from a seed.

guard cells (gärd selz):   cells that surround a stoma and control its size.

gymnosperm (jim′ nə spûrm′):   a seed-bearing plant that produces seeds not protected by a fruit.

herbaceous stem (hûr bā′ shəs stem):   a soft, green stem; xylem and phloem are arranged in bundles.

nonvascular plant (non′ vas′ kyə lər plant):   plant that does not contain xylem and phloem tissue.

osmosis (oz mō′ sis):   the diffusion of water through a membrane.

palisade cells (pal ə sād′):   a layer of loosely packed cells just below the upper epidermis of a leaf that contain chloroplasts.

perennial plant (pə ren′ ē əl):   a plant that lives from one growing season to another; includes all woody stem plants.

petal: the brightly colored leaflike part of flowers that surrounds the reproductive parts.

petiole (pet′ ē ōl′):   a leaf stalk that attaches a leaf blade to the stem.

phloem (flō′ em):   a plant tissue made up of tube-like cells that transports food from the leaves to other parts of the plant.

photoperiodism (fō′ tō pìr′ ē əd iz əm):   the flowering response of a plant to the change in the length of the day.

photosynthesis (fō′ tə sin′ thə sis):   the process in which plants use carbon dioxide and water with light energy to produce food and oxygen.

pigment (pig′ mənt):   a substance that absorbs light.

pistil (pis′ təl):   the female reproductive organ of an angiosperm.

plant behavior: the response of a plant to a stimulus.

pollination (pol′ ə nā′ shən):   the movement of pollen grains from an anther of a flower by wind, water, or animals to a stigma of a flower.

prop root: an aerial root that helps support a plant.

respiration (res′ pə rā′ shən):   the process by which cells release energy from food molecules.

rhizoids (rī′ zoidz):   long, single cells that attach liverworts and mosses to the ground.

root cap: a dome-shaped mass of cells that protects the root as it grows and pushes its way through the soil.

root epidermis (rüt ep′ i dúr′ mis):   the outside covering of a root that comes in contact with the soil; water and dissolved nutrients are absorbed across the root epidermis from the soil.

root hair: a single, threadlike cell that is an extension of the root epidermis; root hairs increase the surface area of the root available for absorbing water and dissolved nutrients.

seed: a plant embryo, stored food, and seed coat.

seed coat: the tough outer layers of a plant ovule.

seed dispersal (sēd di spûr′ səl):   the process of moving plant seeds away from the parent plant.

self-pollination (self pol′ ə nā′ shən):   transfer of pollen grains from stamens to pistils of the same flower or from one flower to another flower of the same plant.

sepal (sē′ pəl):   a leaflike part of a flowering plant that protects the flower when it is a young bud.

sexual reproduction: the fertilization of a female sex cell by a male sex cell.

spongy cells (spun′ jē):   loosely packed cells just inside the lower epidermis of a leaf; they contain chloroplasts.

stamen (stā′ mən):   the male reproductive organ of angiosperms.

stimulus (stim′ yə ləs):   something outside of a plant in its environment that affects the plant's behavior.

stomata (stō mä′ tä):   the slit-like openings or pores in the epidermis of leaves.

taproot (tap′ rüt):   type of root in which food is stored in a long, thick, main root, such as in carrots and beets.

transpiration (tran′ spə rā′ shən):   loss of water by a plant by outward diffusion through the stomata of leaves.

tropism (trō piz əm):   a plant response that involves a change of position by growing toward or away from a stimulus.

vascular plant (vas′ kyə lər):   a plant that contains xylem and phloem tissue.

veins (vānz):   the bundles of xylem and phloem that run through leaves.

woody stem: a hard, rigid stem; the xylem and phloem are arranged in two separate rings—the xylem rings inside the phloem rings.

xylem (zī′ ləm):   a plant tissue made up of vessels that transport water and dissolved nutrients around the plant.

INDEX

CREDITS